# COWBOY CURMUDGEON

## AND OTHER POEMS

Other Cowboy books available from Gibbs Smith, Publisher:

**Cowboy Poetry**
*A Gathering*

**New Cowboy Poetry**
*A Contemporary Gathering*

**Old-Time Cowboy Songs**

**Cowboy Poetry Cookbook:**
*Menus and Verse for Western Celebrations*

**Riders In The Sky**

C2

# COWBOY CURMUDGEON

AND

## OTHER • POEMS

### WALLACE MCRAE

GIBBS·SMITH PUBLISHER

PEREGRINE SMITH BOOKS

SALT LAKE CITY

*Dedication*

For my daughters, Allison and Natalie,
and their mother, Ruth,
my good friends and great critics.

First edition
95 94 93 92   6 5 4 3

Copyright © 1992 by Wallace D. McRae

This is a Peregrine Smith Book, published by
Gibbs Smith, Publisher
P.O. Box 667
Layton, UT  84041

Design by Clarkson Creative
Cover illustration by Jack Hines
Interior illustrations by Clinton McRae

Manufactured in the United States of America

LIBRARY OF CONGRESS CATALOGING-IN-PUBLICATION DATA
McRae, Wallace.
    [Poems.  Selections]
    Cowboy Curmudgeon and Other Poems / Wallace D. McRae
        p.   cm.
    ISBN 0-87905-463-8 (pbk)
    1. Ranch life—Poetry. 2.Cowboys—poetry. I. Title.
PS3563. A3296A6  1992
811'.54—dc20                                        91-37917
                                                   CIP

# CONTENTS

# BOOT SHOPPING

It seemed to me a simple thing since my socks was
    showin' through:
Turn my old boots out to pasture, and buy a pair—brand new.
Well, they built this cowboy K-Mart outa town there in the Mall,
Where I parked my Studdybaker after shippin' drys this fall.
I found the store right easy 'thout gettin' tromped or gored,
And this clerk with a complexion like he'd growed up
    'neath a board
Is a-lurkin' at the boot pile an' he asks me, "Help you, sir?"
Seems he knows that I'm a live one so I answers back, "Why sure."
I tole him that my Hyers, that I'd had for thirty year,
Prob'ly was made faulty.  And at that I seen him sneer,
As he eyeballs how I'm shod.  Then he dimples me a smile,
Says, "I can put you in exotics of the very latest style."
I snorts at his "exotics," tells him, "I'm a Hereford man,
But style sounds right 'cause, sonny, I'm an all-time ranahan."
He starts in crackin' critter skins outa boxes that's absurd.
Why, one has prolapsed puckers like it come off'n a bird!
There's lizzards, snakes and horny toads, crocodiles and eels,
Alligators, sharks; I'm feelin' faint.  I staggers and I reels.
I tells that sucker, "Whoa!  Call off them varmits from yer swamp.
I ain't about to put no foot in things I'm scairt to stomp!"

If yer gettin' yerself reshod, well, pardner, here's a clue,
Avoid them scaly crawlers that'll strike 'r bite 'r chew.
Ask that boot clerk, "Do you carry any kangaroos or camels?
Or somethin' in warm-blooded?  I'm partial t'wards them mammals!"

# WE NEVER RODE THE JUDITHS
FOR IAN TYSON

We never rode the Judiths when we were grey-wolf wild.
Never gathered Powder River, Palo Duro, or John Day.
No, we never rode the Judiths when their sirens preened
 and smiled.
And we'll never ride the Judiths before they carry us away.

Cowboys cut for sign on back trails to the days that used to be
Sorting, sifting through chilled ashes of the past.
Or focused on some distant star, out near eternity,
Always hoping that the next day will be better than the last.

Out somewhere in the future, where spring grass is growing tall,
We rosin up our hopes for bigger country, better pay.
But as the buckers on our buckles grow smooth-mouthed or
 trip and fall
We know tomorrow's draw ain't gonna throw no gifts our way.

And we never rode the Judiths when we were grey-wolf bold.
Never rode the Grande Ronde Canyon out north of Enterprise.
No we never rode the Judiths, and we know we're getting old
As old trails grow steeper, longer, right before our eyes.

My horses all are twenty-some…ain't no good ones coming on.
The deejays and the Nashville hands won't let "…Amazed"
 turn gold.
We're inclined to savor evening now.  We usta favor dawn.
Seems we're not as scared of dyin' as we are of growing old.

I wish we'd a' rode the Judiths when we were grey-wolf wild.
And gathered Powder River, Palo Duro, and John Day.
But we never rode the Judiths when their sirens' songs beguiled
And we'll never ride the Judiths before they carry us away.

# THE COYOTE

If you get back off the interstates
And away from urban trends,
You'll find a coyote doesn't have
A multitude of friends.

But I kind of like to see one,
Or hear him greet the day.
He's sort of part of our old West
That's fading fast away.

Though he demands his tribute
I'll let him have his due.
Let him take his cut, and welcome.
I guess it's his world, too.

# UP NORTH IS DOWN THE CRICK

The rivers and cricks run north 'round here,
So "up north" is down the crick.
This has always seemed to be pretty clear
To any old country hick.

But city folks seem to get confused
Between what's "up" and what's "down."
Elevation is often plumb abused
Causing us rustics to frown.

Now when we say "come up" or "come down,"
We're always quite specific.
But the ups and downs of the folks in town
Are definitely horrific.

When "come over," the country folks say,
They mean across a divide.
But if town people say, "Come over some day,"
You're not sure which way to ride.

There was a time when I was still fair
And had a good attitude.
I said, "Urbanites are only aware
Of a difference in latitude."

But this, like a batch of good theories,
In practice got plumb ate up.
When it was obvious from my queries,
They didn't know down from straight up.

So, work a bit on your "overs" and "ups"
And put some thought on your "downs,"
If you are one of those citified pups
Who don't want to be figgered clowns.

Jist remember up north is down stream,
So up is really down south.
And over always cuts across the seam.
(Cheer up.  Don't be down in the mouth!)

First conjure out which way water goes—
Atlantic-bound, or Pacific.
Then up or down just foller yer nose
Altimetricly specific.

When country bound you'll be thought right smart,
If before you sally forth,
Take the time to memorize this by heart,
Down the crick is always up north.

But up north ain't important a bit,
Compared to how water goes.
Throw your compass in a bottomless pit,
Down's just the way the crick flows.

# THREE DOGS SAT ON THE SIDEWALK

FOR DEAN KOLKA

Three dogs sat on the sidewalk once
    outside the butcher shop
With drooling mouths and pleading eyes,
    but no one deigned to stop
To give them pats or kindly words.
    They lounged there in the street.
They got their share of hostile stares
    but not a shread of meat.
"To hell with this," the town dog said,
    "I'm gonna slip inside,
And steal a steak and eat it
    'til my hunger's nullified."
The ranch dog said, "You go ahead
    and burgle, swipe or steal,
But rustlin' goes again' The Code.
    I won't purloin no meal.
My credit's good down at the bank.
    I got some equity.
I'll get a loan.  I'll go in hock
    to pay the butcher's fee."
The town dog and the ranch dog said,
    "What you gonna do?"
To the third one of their trio,
    a farm dog named Old Lou.
"Ain't gonna steal," Old Lou says,
    "I ain't about to borrow
'Cause either way, you just might pay
    the piper come tomorrow.
If yer lookin' fer a handout,
    here's a trick that works plumb fine
Be patient, look downtrodden,
    but most important: whine."

# THE BELT

My good old belt was getting smooth mouthed
    with a hat-brim curl in back.
Its flower stamp had wilted and
    the buck stitch had a lack
Of stitches.  They had prolapsed
    where I carry my Case knife,
So, "Think I'll get myself rebelted,"
    I says to my good wife.
She says, "I'll buy one for your birthday.
    You go select one at the store."
Well, since she's pickin' up the ticket,
    my expensive tastes just soar.
So it come that every place I go
    I works that whole belt herd.
And, pardner, let me tell you that
    there's belts that's plumb absurd.
There's belts with gromets, studs and lugs
    And beads!  And some that's plain.
There's conchos, and there's biker belts
    that's made of chain saw chain!
There's Indian belts made by some tribe
    in Red Lake, Minnesota,
Some macramed of binder twine
    for them top hands in Dakota.
There's belts that's made of varmit skins,
    the like a' which I never seen.
And farmer belts of belting off a
    pulley-powered machine.
There's some that's twisted outa rawhide,
    or of whorehouse colored hair.
Some say "Your Name," "Your State" (which might be
    one of disrepair).

After sorting through the possibles
    with a keen discerning eye,
Accepting and rejecting all them
    choices, until I
Had this list of belt specs that'd
    cause yer eyes to pop,

With which I strolls in, casual like,
    to Connolly's Saddle Shop
Where I sees my pal, Chas Weldon,
    and I lays out this project.
Says I, "The price is unimportant,"
    before he can object.
"I don't make belts!" Chas Weldon says,
    "I quit 'em long ago."
"You'll make this one," I tells him,
    "Or I'll tell some tales I know."
"Is this blackmail?" Chas Weldon asks.
    "You got her," I reply.
"'N put yer stamp on deep 'n plain
    I want it known that I
Got the last gut binder
    that 'Chuckie Bear' done made."
A blank check that my good wife signed
    on the cash box I then laid.
Now Chuck, he whines and vacillates
    but he finally says okay
'N I got one battle left to win,
    called "Saddle Shop Delay."
He dinks around for quite a while
    but he's beat, and loses heart,
So he gives in 'n builds the belt
    and it's a work of art.
Well, I've had this belt for six months now.
    It suits me to a "T."
And I advertise for my pal, Chuck,
    (who made me swear to secrecy).
"CHAS WELDON MADE THIS BELT FOR ME!"
    in crowded rooms I shout.
But now I got a problem:
    The last hole is egging out.
I s'pose I've gained a pound er two,
    or maybe more than that.
My 501's are shrinkin' too,
    But I ain't gittin' fat!
Old Chuck has had the last laugh,
    the dirty lowlife skunk.
He done won the final battle—
    buildin' me this belt that shrunk.

# A QUIET NIGHT ON THE PRAIRIE

I'm wide awake as a newborn owl,
    staring out bug-eyed at the dark.
Covering up my ears, squelching back tears,
    as my tent mates snore, cough, and bark.

Now Walt kicked her off with his coughing,
    as soon as he rolled out his bed,
And raised me up just like Lazarus
    deep from the slumbering dead.

Then Parkins tuned up with his wheezing…
    come a-charging and barging right in.
Point counterpointing Walt's hacking
    just adding his bit to the din.

My dad (him and me share a bedroll)
    is chasing rabbits in his sleep,
A-whining, snuffing, and growling,
    it's enough to make a kid weep.

Now Ev has joined in the chorus,
    chiming in so sweet and low
With both pitch and volume a-rising
    with his ohh, ohhh, ohhh.

Now here comes the verse.  It's a solo
    that's grating and piercingly sharp.
Who, you ask, is the premier tooth grinder?
    Why it's the great virtuoso, Carp.

Now joins the basso profundo,
    it'll shake you clear to the core.
The tent ropes tremble in sympathy,
    for Duke has commenced to snore.

From a frustrated puddle of sweat,
    I scream out at the sleeping men.
Silence for nearly a four-bar break,
    then they start tuning up again.

First Walt tries out a tentative cough,
    Carp's teeth follow up with a screech,
And the others rush in to fill in the void.
    Their sounds close the brief silent breach.

It's a polycoustic symphony
    that's plumb wondrous in its might.
It crashes, and roars and reverberates
    on and on through an endless night.

You've heard the shrieks of the factory and mill,
    or heard the thunder roar?
But you just don't know what the ruckus is,
    until you have heard Duke snore.

A cat fight in a tin granary
    is like soft rain on the heath,
Compared to old Carp's tuning up
    for some minor grinding of teeth.

Them rock bands make merely a whisper,
    a sonic boom is plumb pleasing,
Compared, if you will, to Walt's coughing,
    or Parkins' casual wheezing.

My dad must have run fifty-odd miles
    in his frantic dreams every night.
And Ev's oh…, ohh…, and ohhhing…,
    would have sent flocks of birds into flight.

Exhaustion at last overtakes me
    about 3:10, or thereabout.
Then promptly at four in the morning
    old Jerry bawls, "Cowboys roll out."

All them folks that rave of the quiet
    in the moonlight out on the plains,
Never spent one night in a bed-tent,
    hearing them nocturnal refrains.

So if you've a craving to suffer,
    or have a masochistic bent
I'd certainly recommend a night…
    or two in a roundup tent.

# THE GRASS-FAT STEERS

Faintly, the east has a hint of a glow;
The Morning Star crystalized, bright and low.
Through the meadow our horses sweep away dew,
Repainting our tracks—a deeper hue.
We will, before the morning's through,
    Load up all the grass-fat steers.

"Easy! Go easy," my dad cautions me.
"Pounds are money, and speed don't come free."
"Roll out, you old devils," I hear off to my side.
"Get hooked up, you rascal, or I'll warp yer hide."
"No, now don't you look back at the Cheyenne divide."
    "Now get up, you grass-fat steers."

Ponderously graceful, the steers hit the trail,
Follow the leader—striding head to tail.
"Take a good look, boy," my dad said to me.
"The times are changing.  You'll no longer see
Big steers trailed to market.  This bunch will be
    The last herd of grass-fat steers."

Surely my dad was funning with me,
But as we rode I could clearly see;
Since the men were strangely quiet and subdued,
Their silence made an eerie solitude.
Perhaps these were, I was forced to conclude,
    The last of the grass-fat steers.

We'd brand in a pen. Calve-out at two.
Retire the carbide. (Windcharges, too.)
We'd ride in a yellow bus to school
And kinda bend, or relax, the Golden Rule.
And maybe think a man was a fool
    To miss those old grass-fat steers.

Decoration Day picnics, down at Lee,
Traded off for electricity;
A new flush toilet, for the house out back
Where snow filtered in through every crack.
Some things made it hard to look longingly back
    To the day of the grass-fat steer.

I know we can't go back, can't regress;
Got to inevitably forge ahead, I guess.
But I wonder: "Where do we go from here?
Are growth and progress really so dear?
If so, then why do I so revere
    The day of the grass-fat steer?"

Oh, we still ride and gather the range.
And some things don't ever seem to change.
A neighbor's word is still pretty good.
And now even city folks gather up wood.
And more and more folks would go back, if they could.
    To the day of the grass-fat steer.

Why, maybe we're headed back to the past,
Where smaller is better, and built to last!
I see bread-loaf stacks are back in style,
And so are gardens, at least for a while.
And I'm a-thinking that maybe I'll
    Go back to those grass-fat steers.

# A WOMAN'S PLACE

FOR KARLA GAMBILL

"A woman's place is in the home." That always has made sense.
They're just not built for riding broncs, nor fixin' barbwire fence.
The "woman's place" is well-defined throughout the cowboy West,
Besides, it's our tradition. Our old ways have stood time's test.
There's lots of things that women do way better than a man.
They're a whiz at washing diapers, or with a frying pan.
Those ladies are a comfort when a man ain't feelin' prime,
So, for cookin' or for lookin', give me a woman every time.
I've always advocated the old values of the West.
I believe, just like gospel, that the old-time rules is best.

A few years back I put things off, like I'm inclined to do.
When branding time come rolling 'round—I didn't have a crew.
And this girl, I'll call her "Laurie," said she'd agree to lend a hand.
I thought she meant her husband! See, I didn't understand
That she meant *her*, you savvy now that I was in a bind.
I didn't want to break her heart. I couldn't be unkind.
She said she had these horses that needed lotsa miles.
I said we'd start at daylight. She says, "Great. And thanks,"
    and smiles.
'Bout three o'clock next morning, while I'm still snoring hard,
I starts, and hears a creeping gooseneck ease into the yard.
We invites her in for breakfast, but she's already ate.
It's an hour and half to daybreak 'n I'm already late.
The crew shows up, but she's the one who gives me an assist
When Old Ranger trys to buck me off. She gathers cows I missed!
While I gees and haws Old Ranger, her horse rolls o'er his hocks. ·
She cuts us cowboys seven ways, 'n does it orthodox.
There ain't nothin' that that girl can't do! I'm feelin' like a dope.
At last in desperation, I says, "Laurie, wanta rope?"
She keeps six rasslers busy. We're all abustin' gut.
She even finds a branded bull that I forgot to cut.
For four long days she shows us how a real hand operates.
She rassles and gives shots and brands. She even "casterates"!
When we gets done I offer up to ride, to pay her back.

In the nicest way that she knows how, she lets me know: I lack
Some basic skills I never learned. My horses ain't the best.
They got more help than they can use. I prob'ly need a rest.

So:

"A woman's place is in the home," to me don't seem so strange,
Because I finally figured Laurie's "Home (is) On The Range."

# GABE FOSTER

I seen Gabe Foster just last week
    one day when down in town.
I recollected when he was
    a rounder of renown.
Drink anything when desp'rate.
    His tastes was broad and deep.
But if you was a-buyin',
    he'd lay off from the cheap
And down prime hooch in double shots.
    He'd grin 'n call you sport
Then say, "My friend is buyin' me
    another little snort."
But if no one was a-buyin'
    his tastes was more abstract,
And he'd drink shaving lotion
    or maybe or'nge extract.
He had this little outfit that
    he'd married some time back.
He'd cuss his wife a-sayin', "Now
    she won't throw me no slack.
Though we been married thirty year
    my name ain't on no deed.
Though I do all the work 'round there
    the missus never seed
That I'm a number one top hand."
    He grins and gives a wink.
"She says she just can't trust no man
    who'd take a little drink.
But she's dead wrong, I ain't addicted
    to no life of booze.
I could quit the bottle anytime,
    quit anytime I choose."
I figured Gabe a hopeless case.
    He'd die a drunken bore
'Cause Gabe could patent sorryness
    and sell it at the store.
Then one day Gabe, he up and quit;
    stayed holed up in the hills.

And never touched another drop,
    nor paid his old bar bills.
I guess he got religion bad;
    relinquished his old ways.
He rages 'round the countryside
    on killin' sin forays,
And carrys on 'bout Demon Rum,
    won't let a man alone.
He's leapfrogged from the gutter up
    on top this iv'ry throne.
Gabe tells us hands "Repent! Repent!"
    and pleads for our confession.
He's offensive, just like always,
    just got a new obsession.

# EMINENT DOMAIN

From the Highland Sod, with faith in God,
To this land, young and profane,
Grandad was drawn, long ere the dawn
Of Eminent Domain.

With no regrets he paid his debts,
Fought the elements to remain.
Each challenge met, long before the threat
Of Eminent Domain.

This land's been wet by my father's sweat.
His bones lie 'neath this plain.
But you'd rip in, with your dust and din,
And Eminent Domain.

My mother's tears and unspoken fears
That she always fought to restrain.
Did she somehow hear, and come to fear
Your Eminent Domain?

"Public need" we're advised to heed,
But it somehow comes out, "private gain."
You play the rune.  Do we dance to the tune
Of Eminent Domain?

You praise to the skies, "Free Enterprise,"
Curse the government as your bane.
But you're quick to use, or even abuse,
Her Eminent Domain.

You pandering blights!  Don't tell me of your rights.
Rights and obligations are twain.
Land's earned by sweat and love—not threat
Of Eminent Domain!

I'll not cower from lines of pipe and power
Or twin scythes of rail for your train.
Understand me full well.  You can go to hell
With your Eminent Domain.

# THE DISPUTED EPICURE

"What's your favorite cut of beef?"
    the highborn lady queried.
Of an old cowboy who long ago
    had grown, both wise and wearied,
Of direct infernal questions
    on the ways of cowpoke lore.
So he considered on this question
    that he'd not been asked before.

With rapt anticipation,
    on his pause, the lady hung.
Until, at last the cowboy said,
    "I'd have to say it's tongue.
Tongue's got flavor 'n texture,
    and nary a bit of bone.
A cinch to cook.  I'd put her up
    on top there, all alone."

Recoiling, the lady said aghast,
    "Surely sir, you jest.
The idea is disgusting.
    Your grossness I protest.
Eat something from out a cow's mouth?
    Your suggestion's crude, I beg."
The cowboy then said softly,
    "Don't s'pose you've ate no egg."

# A CONVERSATION WITH ALBERT

"My predecessors were pioneers,
You see, well over a hundred years
Have passed since John B. lit here, fresh off the Texas trail."
I thought old Albert'd be impressed.
He sorta gazed off t'wards the west
I took that for encouragement, and I went on with my tale.
"The land was young, just like John B.,
The water good, the grass was free.
The Army and the railroad combined to open up the land.
The wolf was here, but the buffalo
No longer wandered to and fro,
So a man could make a living running stock.  You understand?"
Albert nodded, and then he said,
"I understand, you go ahead
And tell me of your hist'ry.  I should learn it," and he smiled.
I said, "The first ones here, they had it best
'Til the grangers came and plowed and messed
The country with their fences; and tamed the land once wild.
Though they were diff'rent, farmers weren't no fools.
They built communities and roads and schools
And churches.  And I guess that has all been for the best.
But they plowed land a man can't trust.
When it got dry, they all went bust.
But they somehow killed the culture of the old-time cowboy West.
Oh, there's still cowboys in picture shows
On the TV tube and at rodeos,
But no one really understands that a way of life was lost.
We got welfare now, and laws and rules
From the government, enforced by fools.
We're losing pride and independence, and that's an awful cost.
We've traded off pride for the role
Of a prostitute.  We're on the dole
Of every give-away program that comes rollin' down the road.
I suppose we realized
That everybody's subsidized
And we dang sure oughta get our share!  Forget the rancher code.
It's been a long time—a hundred years—
But it seems to me, my ancestors' fears
Are coming back to haunt me, and dang it that ain't right.

It's too late in this modern day
We shoulda fought it, back along the way.
Hell, I bet we'd prob'ly won it, if we'd put up a fight!"
"You might," says Albert. "I wouldn't know.
But maybe not.  I gotta go.
So long, and I sympathize with your situation."
With a "See you," and a "You take care"
Albert Tallbull left me standing there.
And drove off nice and easy back to his Reservation.

# ONE MORE SHIPPING DAY

The crew has all been mustered, from around the neighborhood,
A good half hour before the stated time.
The boss had said "six thirty" but every hand there understood
"On time" or "being late" are both a crime.

So we're smoking and we're joking as we idle in the dark,
We've all cinched up and bridled for the ride.
In the eastern sky the only hint of light's the feeble spark,
Of Venus, up above the far divide.

Oh the horses, they are nervous and impatient at the wait.
Each idly restrained by men in chaps.
So they shuffle and they snuffle, test the near rein
 t'wards the gate.
They can smell and hear the cattle in the traps.

Some have caught rotation horses, though the best one
 they've acquired,
For "steady" is the rule of thumb today.
The boss will ride "Old Ready" (We all thought he'd been retired).
It's his final gift to that old mount, I'd say.

You can see the frosty grass now, in the pre-dawn's eerie light
And there's just a hint of light above the hill.
To the west a coyote caterwauls farewell to his friend, Night.
But except for him, and us, the world is still.

It hasn't been no banner year. We didn't get much rain.
But when we needed some, the Lord come through.
Looks as if our outfits'll pay the bills without much strain
If the cattle weigh like we all think they'll do.

To a man, we'd shy away from any show of celebration
Of another round of practicing our art.
Won't be no great orations, there's a proud and choked sensation
In every cowboy's throat and ev'ry heart.

When they cross the scale today, we can carve another notch.
Tally up another year that's filled with pride.

With three wraps and a hooey, drop the flag, read the watch.
Bring on the snow!  We'll take it all in stride.

The boss's caught the stirrup.  Ready's ears are at attention.
In my mind I hear a piper far away.
Another day, another dollar.  The sun is making its ascension.
We're mounting up, for one more shipping day.

# RANCH WIFE

It's hard to be a ranch wife
And be a fashion plate.
Hoein' weeds and hangin' wash
Don't tend to cultivate
Soft hands or clear complexions,
Or a stunning silhouette.
Sun-ravaged hair don't tend to make
A ravishing coquette.

But there is beauty unsurpassed
By all the gatefold girls,
Of all the beauty-pageant queens
With teased and coiffured curls.
Like the beauty of filled canning jars,
A wreath made of fresh pine,
The glowing faces of ranch kids,
Dried sheets, fresh from the line.

There's a loveliness in rough, stained hands
Making jelly from wild plums.
The simple tears of pain or grief
When birth or death each comes.
So don't sing to me of goddesses
Larger (and falser) than life.
Or denegrate the beauty
Of the solid, strong ranch wife.

# MAGGIE

I taught my good dog, Maggie,
"Lay down," when I commanded.
I also taught her "Set,"
Whenever I demanded.

"I'll teach her now to speak," said I.
She labored to comply.
And when she learned to speak she said,
"You twit, it's 'sit' and 'lie!'"

# THE HOMESTEAD HOUSE

The old homestead house with the door askew.
Windows stare dully at the prairie view.
You're all that remains, the grey residue,
Of dreams, and work, and a vision that grew
Into a nightmare of debts overdue.

Who was it that labored here, Fritz, or Frieze?
It makes no difference in times like these.
Once here, now you're gone like the fitful breeze.
Did your dreams burn away?  Or did they freeze?
What unknown gods did you fail to appease?

What homeland produced you?  German or Swede?
Johnson, or Jackson, Kaharski, or Snead?
Of no consequence now, who hoed the weed,
Who borrowed and saved to purchase the seed,
And grimly forced, in the end, to concede.

Refugee of the city, store, or mill,
Forced on by greed, by sheer terror, or will;
The hope of credit and granaries to fill…
Did you look back, as you left o'er the hill?
Did you cry in anguish?  Or was your voice still?

Who was the culprit?  And who should we hate?
Was it the railroad, the banks, or just fate?
Was it the program to settle the state?
Did someone purposely prevaricate?
Or your own suffering did you create?

Questions unanswered, I ride as before,
Leaving the house with the sagging front door.
First Indian, then settler, was at the fore.
Am I the next to be swept from the floor
Of the plains?  My ranch to ride nevermore?

As I cross the draw, beside a plowshare,
I see a stone spearpoint just lying there.
Should I leave a piece of cowboy hardware?
That would, with their relics, spatially share;
To remind those coming, that we were there?

Let the spearpoint stay there yet for a while.
They'll not bury the plow 'neath a spoil pile.
This ground of "ours" I'll not let them defile,
Damn their threats and their attempts to beguile.
I'll cast off no spur embracing exile.

# EXODUS

"There was this preacher told this story,"
An old cowpoke told his friend,
"And tho I've conjured on it some
I ain't sure I comprehend."

"It's about this feller, Faro, and
This Moses, his hired hand,
And this sage-and-gumbo outfit
In this place called He-Gyped-Land."

"It seems this Moses was a-workin'
For barely grub and bed,
When the Lord rode in from Heaven
And his howdys was all said,
'How's things a-goin' for ya?'
The Lord ast this Moses hand.
'She's awful tough,' says Moses,
'For us here in He-Gyped-Land.
The outfit's boss, old Faro?
Well, he's rougher than a cob.
Us hands'd like to mosey on
And find another job.
Ya see, we'd like to roll our beds
And hit out for our home range.
Our pickin's here is mighty slim,
So, we're relishin' a change.
But Old Faro he won't let us quit.
He won't write us out our check.
He's got these pyramids to build,
Which don't thrill us a speck.
While he louts around in fancy duds
There in his palacial house,
Eatin' steak and drinkin' gin,
We're sorrier than a louse.
We hear the stages and railroads
Is owned by Mr. Faro,
And he won't let us ride on them,
Which seems to me plumb narrow.
We don't have no horse a-tall,
Or we'd ride off some dark night.
We're just like slaves!' said Moses,
'And you know that that ain't right!' "

"Well, the Lord He weighed and pondered some,
Then He said, 'Well, I agree.
He sure ain't treated you folks right,
I'm a-gonna set you free.
I'll set some plagues on Faro;
...Change a stick into a snake.
While he is throwed plumb off his leads,
You hands can make your break.'
'But Faro's hired these fast gun hands,'
The pleading Moses said.
'And they'll ride out and fetch us back,
'Fore we cross the River Red.'
The Lord, He fires right back at Moses,
'You just gather up your band.
I'll fix them guns and Faro, too.
Pack up!  You understand?' "

"A cloudbust turned the cricks blood red,
Way too muddy fer a drink,
That killed the fish and pollywogs
And they commenced to stink.
The Lord gathered flocks of horned toads
Which swarmed out across the land.
They holed up inside Dutch ovens,
And bedrolls, I understand.
The cows and calves they all got lousy
(And likewise folks, I guess),
And face flies come in swarmin' clouds,
It was an awful mess.
Them lousy cows got anaplaz
(or it mighta been red nose),
And fistuloes, and lumps, and boils
From their backs down to their toes.
It hailed the grass and greasewood
Down to little bitty nubs.
And killed antelope and mule deer
Like they was hit with clubs.
Then come hoards of Mormon Crickets,
(And the grasshoppers, their kin)
Till not a livin' thing was left
Where knee-high grass had been."

"Well, Moses led the gitaway
(Just like the Lord had said).
A flash flood nailed Old Faro's guns
While crossin' the River Red."

"Well that there's the tale the preacher told,
Just as near as I recall.
So whatcha think?" the cowpoke asked,
"Ya s'pose it's true a-tall?"

The cowpoke's friend rolled up a smoke
And spit into the fire
Then said, "It ain't my nature
To call no man a liar
An' I'd be the first one to admit
There's some I don't understand.
Like Moses bein' set afoot
If'n he was such a hand.
But all them things that happened there,
You surely do agree,
Has all been seen by me and you,
And just differ in degree."

That said, he stoked the fire up
And gave his pal a pat,
Saying, "Me and you has cowboyed
Fer outfits worse'n that.
That there country sounds like Texas,
And the best part, I allow.
Wisht I knowed old Faro's address
And if he's hirin' now."

# OLD SPEED AND TWO MILK COWS

Thinking today of those long lost days
Refocused clearly through years of haze
How old was I then?  Maybe five or six.
With a quantum leap from pretend-horse sticks
To rawhidin' wrangler of mavericks…
Gathering two milk cows.

"Gotta learn some time," my father said.
"He'll hang up and drag," said Mom with dread.
Negotiations, with shouts and sighs,
I overhear, and I agonize.
"He'll ride bareback," was the compromise,
Wrangling two milk cows.

With nonchalant halter I'd trap old "Speed."
The old oat glutton, finessed by greed,
Became Pegasus or Man of War;
The steed of a knight whose lance dripped gore,
Or the Marshal's, out to settle the score,
Challenging two milk cows.

Barefooted kid on a bareback horse
Learning the rules as a matter of course:
"You choused those cows," my dad'd say.
"Trotted cows give butter or cheese and whey."
"But they made a move to get away,
Crazy old milk cows."

"You never cut those old milk cows slack.
Rest of the week you can walk, footback.
Old Speed and the cows could both stand some rest
And you need to learn how a cow goes best.
Now pick up your lip, it's hittin' your chest."
"Damn those two milk cows!"

So day by day, as I made a hand,
A hand was made.  Now I understand
A-looking back before learning to read,
I learned some lessons that I still heed
From my dad, and a plug by the name of Speed,
And two brindle, slow milk cows.

# COFFEE

The feller who invented coffee
Rates pretty high in my book.
You could prob'ly run the Tongue for a week
With the gallons that I've partook.

Sawyers, Butternut or Hills Brothers
Arbuckle or MJB,
Them old brands, and a whole batch of others,
Has been sipped and savored by me.

From a bucket done in the camp fire,
Or porcelain cup in town,
It's all good, but some of it's better—
A-steamin' and velvety brown.

Cream or sugar?  No thanks.  Black's for me,
And strong.  Yep, hotter than Hell.
Them contented chemists' Dixie-cup cream
Don't really suit me too well.

Some day when I turn hoofey-side up,
Joinin' Hell's (or St. Peter's wing'd ranks),
I'll work the herd for coffee's inventor,
To give him a Howdy,…and Thanks.

# WINTER MOISTURE

Got this neighbor, a fusser and a fretter,
Says he'd sure like to have it some wetter.
Though it's twenty below,
He's been yearnin' for snow;
Tempting fate.  And he oughta know better.

So it snowed, shrouding hummock and tuffet,
Two feet deep, and we'll all have to rough it.
Sure hope he got his share.
Since I got some to spare,
I can tell him just where he can stuff it!

# "I KNOWED OLD CHARLIE WELL"

Time was when every old-timer
When storying-up a spell
Would look you squarely in the eye
Saying, "I knowed 'Kid' Russell well."

Men that'd never misrepresent
A critter they had to sell,
Would often casually mention,
"I knowed Charlie Russell well."

The Mint couldn't hold the 'punchers
Who'd drone like a funeral knell
Of drinks they'd shared with them boys
Who all knowed old Charlie so well.

They all "once had a pitcher of Charlie's,
But sold it when 'short' for a spell.
'When Horses Talk War' it was titled,
And I knowed Old Charlie damn well."

The Devil must just love old Charlie
As he pitchforks them cowboys 'round Hell
That never lied 'bout nothin' else
'Cept for knowin' Charlie so well.

# HAT ETIQUETTE

There are rules of decorum and conduct
    to which genuine cowboys attest.
Call them mores, traditions or manners,
    they're part of the code of the West.
But cowpokes have got this dilemma,
    that confuses these sage diplomats.
It involves the whens and when-not-tos,
    concerning the wearing of hats.
The old rule concerning head covers says
    "Hat-up when you work, or you ride.
Tip 'em to women. But take John B. off
    when in bed, or when you're inside."
But whaddya do in a gin mill,
    bean shops or dances in town?
Where Resistol rustlers'll filch it
    or some low-life'll puke in its crown.
'N there ain't no such thing as a hat rack
    anyplace that I been of late.
So we all compromise with a tip back,
    baring pallid foreheads and bald pate.
What we needs is a new resolution
    to settle this conflict we got.
So I come up with this here solution,
    a result of consider'ble thought:
"I move that we do like good Hebrews,
    wear hats from our birth 'til we die.
And never remove them sombreros.
    All those in favor say, 'Aye.'"

# BROKE, AFOOT AND OLD

He'd prob'ly heeled ten thousand calves
And rode a million draws.
He'd sacked out a hundred broncs
And broke some rank outlaws.

He maybe knowed a critter's mind
Some better than they did.
He started pluggin' after 'em,
When he was just a kid.

He tied a hundred fiadores.
Wore out a dozen rigs.
He forked his share of cold jaws,
Or ones with eyes like pigs.

But he had rode some good ones, too,
More, maybe, than his share.
If they had hair he'd ride 'em
(Unless they was a mare).

He never seemed to take much note
Of how a country lay.
But ranges he rode years ago
He recollects today.

"One of the best, I was," he says
(As he bums me for a smoke),
"One of the very best, but
I'm old, afoot and broke."

His stained and gnarled fingers clutch
A shaking double shot.
His eyes plead for another
To match the one I bought.

He rides his range in memory
His flick'ring fire grows cold.
I ease away. My eyes fill.
He's broke, afoot, and old.

# BILL SEWARD, KING OF THE JERSEY LILLY

Jersey Lilly's a sort of a hole in the wall.
"Best place in town," its advocates bawl,
"And for miles around, it's the best bar by far."
(Ain't no place nowhere near Ingomar.)
    Bill Seward's the King of it all.

You can tie up your mount to the Lilly's hitch rack.
'Round the sunny side's two sheds out back.
One's labeled "Bucks," t'other one "Does,"
Which's where one goes whenever one "goes."
    Bill Seward's is no yuppie shack.

She's a droughty country 'round Ingomar,
Water all come from a railroad car.
When the Milwaukee Road went plum to hell
Folks throwed t'gether t' drill 'em a well
    'N t' water Bill Seward's bar.

Bill Seward's liberal with a back-bar quart,
But he remembers when water was short.
'N Bill thinks water's for doin' dishes.
"Ain't made to drink 'less yer fishes,"
    Bill Seward'll say with a snort.

Bill's nose is this wide, or maybe more,
From boxin' back in the Second World War.
"Middleweight Champ a' the whole dang fleet,"
He'll show you clippings.  They tell who he beat.
    Bill Seward don't fight no more.

He serves beef and beans in his Jersey Lilly
In his sailor hats some'd think was silly
With the hangy-down holdin'-up-eyeglass-string,
But nobody makes of it no big thing…
    (Bill whipped that club champ from Philly.)

So if you get up on the North Side 'n say
Got a minute er two, or most of a day,
'N yer thirsty 'r gant 'r Republican,
Jersey Lilly's the place, 'n Bill's yer man.
    Bill Seward?  He savvys the Cowboy Way.

So tie up yer hoss, 'r park yer car
(Sure it's out of the way.  Most good places are!)
Just take a trip back in time and space
To some good cowboys' favorite place
    Where Bill Seward's King of the Bar.

# COMMUTED SENTENCE

Now there's got to be a reason
(although I'm not sure why),
Whenever he is seen or heard
A rattlesnake must die.
Some rumor of a calf or colt
Who died back in the past,
Dictates to all: this creature must
Be killed—a vile outcast.
Or the taint from Eden's Garden
Residual in man's mind,
Sans jury, judge, or legal aid,
Says "kill" to all mankind.
For years I've packed their rattles home,
And filled a Mason jar.
'Cause I've never ridden by them,
Or left them where they are.
But some day when no one's looking
My reason will hold sway,
And I'll bid a rattler "Howdy,"
And grin and ride away.

# ANOTHER COWBOY

FOR JUSTIN WAGNER

To the top of his ears, his hat's jerked down.
There's an old-time crease in its dusty crown.
He knows the score and the culture's rules
And suffers insufferable frauds and fools
With inscrutable eyes below brim-covered frown.
He patiently watches life's tales unfold.

He don't say much.  It's not that he's shy.
He's watching, and judging, the world going by
As he hunkers down on dusty boot heels,
Sifting and sorting the emotions he feels
As the other hands preen and prophesy
With studied poses and stories bold.

He's away from the ranch and chores and care
Behind the chutes at the county fair.
He's seen the fed steers and 4-H hogs;
Heard the carnies prattle like demagogs.
Now he judges the buckles the roughstockers wear
Adding to or subtracting from narratives told.

The hands josh him a bit.  He smiles at the joke.
Shakes his head, "no thanks," to a chew or a smoke.
He knows his place.  He's satisfied there
On the rim of the circle the bronc riders share.
Though a bit out of sync, he's sure 'nuff cowpoke.
His time's a-comin'.  His story's not told.
The torch'll be passed. He's eight years old.

# AN OUNCE OF PREVENTION

Eggs'll give you fatty heart.
Beef'll plug your veins.
Booze'll make your liver hard
'N give you kidney pains.

Pop'll make your teeth rot out.
Same with sweets and gum.
Chocolate'll give you pimples
Which makes your love life glum.

Coffee'll make you nervous.
Beans'll give you gas.
Pot'll curdle up your genes
Or cook your pancreas.

Snoose'll rot your lower lip
Or make your teeth fall out.
Drink some beer?  Eat rich food?
You're sure to get the gout.

Smokes'll cause lung cancer.
Cheese'll constipate.
But prunes'll make you scour some
And make your tum gyrate.

Saccharin'll give you tumors.
Cyclamates'll too.
Red dye'll stain your innards
And give you Green Gomboo.

Salt'll boost blood pressure up.
Pepper makes you sneeze.
Florides freckle up your teeth
And knobby-up your knees.

Pork'll give trichinosis
Which makes your muscles balk.
Rabbit'll "tootleream" you
Or cause your jaws to lock.

Everything is dangerous.
Some more and some less.
So don't partake of nothin'
And you won't die…I guess.

# IN QUEST OF THE FESTIVE BOUGH

It's getting down deep in December.
Time to work the herd for a tree.
So after doing the feeding, the family
Climbs in the pickup with me.

Now I don't know 'bout your household,
But mine's sure ain't easy to please.
I've got this plethora of critics
When it comes to judging them trees.

Jackpine, cedar or plum bush?
It don't really matter to me.
I'd just cut the first one I come to
Though it weren't no symmetrical tree.

Them critics of mine got to wrangle
And measure, argue and talk
Of breadth, depth and thickness,
So we walk, we walk, and we walk.

Of course every dang sylvan candidate
Is clear at the top of the hill.
And though, "Those don't look so good up close,
Those over there prob'ly will."

I straggle along with an axe and a saw
Cussin' Santy Claus with each step.
While the critics' derision and scorn
Is only surpassed by their pep.

See all them tracks a-milling around
Where the family skidded and larked?
We finally come back to the pickup
And cut one, right where we was parked.

# OL' PROC

Old-timers in the neighborhood
Would bandy words on who was good
At puncher jobs for hours on end when I was just a kid.
They'd get wall-eyed 'n paw and bawl
And swear, "By damn I knowed 'em all.
If'n Josh he wasn't best trailhand, I'll eat my beaver lid!"

"Down and dirty, I'm the dealer.
Old Bob Seward?  Best damn peeler
Ever snapped a bronc out, jist give me one he broke."
"Give, you say?  That's what I heard.
You're right that Bob's a tough ol' bird.
But better practice cactus pickin' and work on your spur stroke.

Cain't stay astraddle one of his'n
When he pops the plug and goes t' fizzin'
She'll be adios caballo and howdy to the nurse."
They'd move from bickering bronc peelers
To rawhide hands 'n fancy heelers.
"Red Carlin?"  "Young Mac Philbrick?"  They'd testify and curse.

They'd analyze Link Taylor's cuttin':
"His bag-splittin' way of calf denuttin'
Is pure askin' for trouble, 'sides he don't cut by the sign."
"You cut your calves by the moon?
Keep on night brandin' and pretty soon
The sheriff'll change yer address and you'll be twistin' hair
    and twine."

On they'd rave and postulate
'Bout who was fair 'n who was great.
As they scratched brands in the hot dust, I'd never say a word.
But in their jousting verbal battle,
Among the boasts and barbs and prattle,
I sat in youthful judgment as they sorted out the herd.

So I came early to understand
The names of every good top hand.
In my scope of country, from hearing tough hands talk.
But when they'd crow and blow and boast
The one name that came up the most
Was a wily wild horse runner they simply called "ol' Proc."

"You boys jist start 'em.  I'll stop 'em."
Old Proc'd say and then he'd chop 'em
Off at some escape route.  He'd wheel 'n bring them in.
"Proc thinks horse," I'd heard them say,
And finally there came the day
That I would get to meet this fabled mounted paladin.

My mother's father, John McKay,
Up and said one fine spring day
While I was staying with them, "Minnie, get your bonnet."
"Let's go up by the Castle Rock
'N see some country, visit Proc.
If you're late, I'll be upset.  You can bet your life upon it."

He never paused for her reply.
My grandma fussed around and I
Asked grandpa, "Is he the wild horse man?"  "That's him,"
    my grandpa said.
As we ricocheted and bounced our way
In a tobacco-stained green Chevrolet
My grandpa told "Proc stories" and chewed and spit and sped.

From all the tales Grandpa told me
I felt like an authority
On this ranahan, Joe Proctor, who came north with Texas cattle.
His wife had been the JO cook.
But Proc had sparked and won and took
Her for his bride.  They fought and won the homestead battle.

I couldn't wait to meet Mr. Proc,
Whose peers all praised his ways with stock.
But when his calloused hand gripped mine, surprise hit me
    in waves.
Those old cowboys who cut no slack
Deemed it unimportant Proc was black,
And wasn't worth a mention that Joe Proctor's folks were slaves.

# TELEPHONE CALL

"Did I gitcha up?...Well I'm sorry.
    Don't wanta throw ya in no dang bind.
But, you see, I been thinkin' 'bout dyin'.
    Yah, it's sorta been there in my mind.
Well, I've had these episodes lately,
    'n hell, kid, I'm seventy-five.
I want to pick me a burial plot—
    long as I'm still alert 'n alive.
Now, I didn't call up for your pity,
    'n I don't want you takin' it hard,
But I figgered that you was in charge now
    of your grandad's local graveyard.
When did John B. deed it over?
    You say back in nighteen aught two?
And who'd be the first one they put there?
    Well now, he'd be an uncle to you.
Hell, you know that.  I'm gettin' forgitful
    'n lately, I sometimes black out.
'N the doctors, well, they can't find nothin'.
    The old lady keeps stewin' about
Me not wantin' to lay with the vet'rins.
    Yah, you aughta hear old Iness rage
When I tells her I wants t' lay under
    the cactus, bluejoint and sage.
Speakin' on sage, you remember once back
    in the Second World War
How yer mom sent that sprig of fresh sagebrush?
    It wore out, I ain't got it no more.
Last Tuesday I come in all muddy; my shirt was all
    smeared with grass stains.
When I come to, my horse was a-grazin'
    a ways off, a-draggin' the reins.
Well, I got to thinkin' of Egan,
    yer dad Don, Elmore, and the rest,
Of all them old hands I rode with,
    By God, kid, I rode with the best!
Weren't you there when we branded on Rye Grass?
    Now, ain't thought a' that for a while.

Outside! we was.  Old Ev never missed,
   now there was a heeler with style!
Old Carp got bucked off!  The bed-tent blowed down!
   And Chauncy, the cook, he got drunk!
...The old lady says to git off'n the phone.
   Says I'm borin' you with this junk.
So I'll come on down 'n pick me a plot.
   This old hoss has about run his race.
By chance if I don't, you pick me a spot
   in some out-of-the-way sort of place.
You bet.  Same to you.  Take care of yourself.
   Drop in if you git up this way.
I might tell you some stories to write pomes about.
   So long then.  See ya some day."

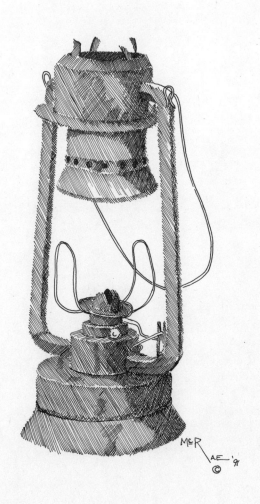

# THE LAND

Gestating in the mid-year
Seldom did it show.
Youthful green in springtime.
White, and gaunt with snow.

She who each year faithfully
Gives her produce away,
Never asking compensation,
Quiet, unassuming is her way.

You'd ravish her with mindless lust,
Then curse her for a whore.
You've never loved her as I have,
Or you'd respect her more.

Rip open her hard belly.
Tear her vitals out.
Sew her back with zippered tracks
That wander roundabout.

You'd prostitute her beauty
With cosmetic care.
Strip her of fertility
And leave her prostrate there.

# REINCARNATION

"What does reincarnation mean?"
A cowpoke ast his friend.
His pal replied, "It happens when
Yer life has reached its end.
They comb yer hair, and warsh yer neck,
And clean yer fingernails,
And lay you in a padded box
Away from life's travails."

"The box and you goes in a hole,
That's been dug in the ground.
Reincarnation starts in when
Yore planted 'neath a mound.
Them clods melt down, just like yer box,
And you who is inside.
And then yore just beginnin' on
Yer transformation ride."

"In a while, the grass'll grow
Upon yer rendered mound.
Till some day on yer moldered grave
A lonely flower is found.
And say a hoss should wander by,
And graze upon this flower,
That once wuz you, but now's become
Yer vegetative bower."

"The posy that the hoss done ate
Up, with his other feed,
Makes bone, and fat, and muscle
Essential to the steed.
But some is left that he can't use,
And so it passes through,
And finally lays upon the ground.
This thing, that once wuz you."

"Then say, by chance, I wanders by,
And sees this on the ground.
And I ponders, and I wonders at,
This object that I found.
I thinks of reincarnation,
Of life, and death, and such.
I come away concludin': 'Slim,
You ain't changed, all that much.'"

# DEGREES OF WATER

"A good year," all the ranchers say.
"There's worldsa grass 'n lotsa hay."
"A good strong inch we got last week."
"My dams is full; likewise the creek."
Cowmen repeat the old refrain:
"You can cuss the mud, but not the rain."

"She's mighty tough," the ranchers say.
"We're s'posed to get more snow today."
"You tell me, what the hell good's grass
That's under snow up to your ass?"
"Them cows can't get a decent drink.
Each water hole's a skating rink."

The molecule the ranchers know,
That's critical, is $H_2O$.
But cows get thinner, or get fatter,
Depending on a state of matter.
Fates and fortunes ebb and flow
Based on rates of rain, or snow.
We're "belly up," or "got it made,"
By water measured…centigrade.

# THE CLINCHER

He looked like the consummate cowboy.
Said he was both born, and ranch bred.
He talked of all of the outfits he'd rode
But he put his hat on a bed.

He spoke of all the rodeos he'd worked,
Of buckles won in his riding career,
From Calgary to Texas, from east to west
But he turned wrong-way to a steer.

He told us of all the roundups he'd repped.
How they'd trailed this and that bunch to the train.
Of the wagon he'd bossed down Mexico way
Then wrote on the tent in the rain.

He had silver bits, and tack of all kinds
Cached away in his bedroll.
He'd packed and wrangled all over the West
But tied his horse to the tent pole.

To any doubts cast at the stories he told,
He laughed them away as absurd.
I'd almost decided he might be legit
When he rode between me and the herd.

# WHAT KIND OF AN OUTFIT YOU GOT?

"She's as good a country as lays outdoors."
You'll hear it all over the West.
The platitudinal rhetoric soars,
Wherever they're from is the best.

Oh, the skies there are always the bluest.
The grass, though it's sparse, wondrous strong.
Their neighbors and friends are the truest.
And droughts never last very long.

You betcha there's plenty of water.
Each BLM hand is a pard.
Noxious weeds stay away like they oughter.
Ain't no dandelions in his yard.

He's never known one rustling suspect.  Not one!
His real estate taxes are low.
There's team-roping practice each Sunday for fun.
Soft breezes blow balmy and slow.

Trophy bucks graze each canyon and swale.
Hungry fish lurk in shaded pools deep.
His ranch?  It just happens to be up for sale.
Buy it quick and he'll let 'er go cheap.

# OUR COMMUNION

*He said, "This bread's my body."*
*He said, "My blood's the wine.*
*Remember when you take it,*
*The blood and body's mine."*

Our bodies are this fertile land.
This water is our blood.
Our plains form our communion.
Our god's organic mud.

Your blasting rends our very flesh.
Your mining cuts our veins.
Our fly-blown, bloating bodies
Lie piled upon the plains.

You'd load our bones on somber
Black, unit funeral trains.
Or burn them in cremation
Pyres.  Dachaus of the plains.

By callous men, and greedy,
Our deaths unsanctified.
A region, and its people,
Both being crucified.

Proffer up the other cheek?
Our cries should we subdue?
Say, "Forgive them, Father, for
They know not what they do?"

Should we ignore the spectre
Of this base incubus?
As they debauch our country
Do they ever think of us?

The water is our life-blood.
Our bodies are the land.
Why can't they comprehend this?
Why don't they understand?

# RED PUP, BONINE, AND OWL

I go to some horse shows every year,
And usually come home feeling foul,
And slightly ashamed of my stay-at-home mounts:
Red Pup, Bonine, and Owl.

The arena horses are shining and proud.
Their ears are always alert.
While Red Pup, Justin, Balley, and Snip
Are slovens, in sweat and in dirt.

Cutting horses dance a delicate step.
The haltered ones stand as if frozen.
While Justin and Balley stand hipshot, ears down,
Fightin' flies, and a-dozin'.

Pleasure horses lope with infinite grace.
Their riders sweep by so erect.
Owl's favorite gait is a jog that would not
Win any prize, I suspect.

But could the show horses keep up with my boys,
Doing their chores on the ranch?
Could they make the circle, work herd, drag the calves?
Would an honest day's work make them blanch?

Red Pup, and Bonine, you suit me just fine.
I'm not one of the horse-showing crowd.
But when we've had things on the ranch to get done,
You always have done yourselves proud.

So Hail! to the Red Pups, the Bonines, and Owls.
Hail! to the equine wage slave.
In this beholder's eye you're beauties.
You never took as much as you gave.

# ZACK TILMAN

They say his dad was bone-deep mean;
    his ma had ceased to care.
His sisters quit their home range
    and they scattered everywhere,
Wherever neon glittered
    and booze and life was cheap.
So off Zack slipped one dark night
    while the old man was asleep.
He hitched a ride to Idaho
    where one sister was a whore.
"Naw, she's not here," the madam said.
    "Been gone six months, or more."
An old mustanger coming through
    from down Nevada way
Said he could use a maverick kid
    his keep would be his pay.
They gathered up the mustang bands
    and lived light off the land.
Till some buckaroos and ranchers
    began to understand
They didn't own the beef they ate
    nor was it store-bought
Nor did they check for brands real close
    on cayuses they caught.
Now when the law came sniffin' 'round
    the old man never bent.
They shot him down, as young Zack watched
    just outside their tent.
"Be tough," the old man taught him,
    "You gotta learn t' fight."
At "School for Boys" young Zack learned quick
    the old man was dead right.
Zack never shed another tear.
    He never took no guff.
He learned his bitter lessons well,
    got lean and mean and tough.
Zack rode the rough strings here and there,
    all up and down The West.

Old connoisseurs of cruelty
    still claim "Zack was the best."
He stormed the weekend rodeos,
    or so old hands relate.
A surgeon, with his locked-spur rowels,
    on stock he'd operate.
The forties came, and young Zack learned
    some crafts not used before;
He honed his skills at killing
    in the South Pacific War.
He'd finally found his place in life,
    new talents were refined,
But then they up and told him
    that an armistice was signed!

He scorned the peacetime army;
    jeered their proffered "bars."
And only missed the battlegrounds,
    grenades and BARs.
Now most men think that war's a curse,
    a sojourn down in Hell.
But war to Zack was heaven-sent;
    a job that he did well.
A hero—semicivilized—
    Zack was, when he got back.
He went to GI Bill trade schools
    and sorta found the track
Of normal life.  He sparked and won
    an old-time rancher's prize.
He beat her until finally
    she came to realize
That though his love for her was strong
    he'd prob'ly take her life.
She left him.  But he always claimed
    "the bitch" was still his wife.
He fought with neighbors constantly
    and shot their stock for spite.
Some say he torched a neighbor's hay
    when they were gone one night.
He picked a hundred fights in bars.
    He'd push, then take offense

And beat a murder rap one time
    by claiming self-defense.
Soon every one was terrorized.
    He couldn't find a fight.
He finally found his enemy
    and killed himself one night.

# OLD BLUFFER

I've long had to suffer you boys cussin' old Bluffer;
Good a pup as a feller could own.
But let me tell you a story that's both grim and gory
When that cow dog's true colors was shown.
Once old Bluffer 'n me is rawhidin' you see
Fer a cow that is shelly and old.
She's twelve year past her youth 'n ain't got a tooth
In her head and she can't take the cold.
She's lousy as well so this last arctic spell
Will for sure turn her titty-side up.
So we're pokin' around, searchin', coverin' ground,
Me, my hoss and old Bluffer, my pup.
As we're sicklin' along, I'm hummin' some song
Then my hoss hits a hole hid by snow.
There's no time to get loose. I swaller my snoose.
Somethin' pops when we land and I know
That for sure it's a leg—been smashed like some egg.
But whose leg?  My horse's or mine?
Then I guess I passed out.  Comin' to—ain't no doubt—
Pony's gone.  I'm alone.  Then a whine
From old Bluffer, my pard, who's been there standin' guard
And I'm thankful that I ain't alone.
Well old Bluff licks my chin 'n wags me a grin
Then I move and I stifle a moan.
I'm gittin' cold and I quiver.  The pain sends a shiver
And I pass out again for a spell.
When I come up for air that good dog is still there
But my future looks shorter than hell.
As the waves of pain rage, I tear out a page
From my faithful old worn tally book,
And I carefully write a note of my plight
And location where searchers should look.
With my wild rag I waller old Bluffer a collar
And I carefully tie on my note.
I don't give him no choice.  In my no-nonsense voice
"Bluff!  Go home!"  Said with tears in my throat.
Can you guess the rest of old Bluff's hero test?
Well sir, you can all see I ain't dead,
But I find myself wishin' I could shed this suspicion

I got rollin' around in my head.
When them boys cut my track, 'n brought me on back
Almost out of sight they found Bluffer
Right there by the trail a-waggin' his tail
Curled up, restin', watchin' me suffer.

# THE OLD MEN IN THE LOBBY

The old men in the lobby,
Their frames are lean and spare.
They stare and wait expectantly,
Each in his own chair.
They judge like black-robed justices,
In court, beneath the stair.
Their verdict's always, "Guilty"—
Consistent, if not fair.

The old men in the lobby
Wear expressions wary.
Their rounded backs and stringy legs
Bespeak the loads they carry.
Is the load a long-dead love
They did, or didn't marry?
The crushing load of coming death
That grows, as here they tarry?

The old men in the lobby,
Were they ever young?
Did they once grasp the keg of life,
And gulp wine from its bung?
Did they join the raucous song,
As loudly it was sung?
Or vault life's swaying ladder
To the highest giddy rung?

The old men in the lobby,
Were they always old?
And always on the sidelines
Viewing battles, bold?
For safety, and complacency,
Was all adventure sold?
Were they once flushed with passion,
Or always grey, and cold?

The old men in the lobby
Watch life show its lies.
Stoically they survey it
With baleful, rheumy eyes.
What are the secrets that they hold,
As they gurgle, burp, and sigh?
Some day, too soon, I'll understand,
When an old grey man am I.

# GRANDMOTHER'S FRENCH HOLLYHOCKS

They were probably planted there by the gate
Or along the fence of the watergap lot
Where the milk cows lazed and the work teams ate
Chicken-wired out of the garden plot.

Why! didn't she know they'd scatter around?
Their seeds infecting our vegetable garden.
Magenta blooms fought for fertile ground
Crowding and choking, begging no pardon

Of the carrots or beets in militant rows,
Cut down by the shrapnel of Gaulish genes,
From ambush, they fell like dominoes.
In retreat we skirmished to save the beans

For the canning jars, waiting empty and green,
Wide mouthed as grackles with demanding maws,
That would nourish during months snowy and lean,
When the hunger moon, grinning, flexed grizzled jaws.

"Foolish woman!" we thought, to be tempted by beauty.
"What could she be thinking?" so all of us said.
Our lives bound by the iron bands of duty,
Not frivolous flowers! Just beans, beef and bread.

Of course no one complained, not to her face.
She surely repented the sin of her ways.
Her silent apology mitigated disgrace,
But the shame of her weakness she bore all her days.

She was guilty, of course. More guilty were we.
For beauty in life has strong healing powers.
Fifty years later, I'm beginning to see
The value of Grandmother's beautiful flowers.

# OUTRIDERS AT THE END OF THE TRAIL
## DEDICATED TO THE MEMORY OF MY UNCLE EVAN D. McRAE

They contemplate their town-boot toes
As they stand around and mill.
They check the south horizon,
'Cross the tracks above the hill.
Their suitcoats hint of mothballs.
Their Levis are clean and creased.
They speak of grass or cattle
But never the deceased.
Some have shook the Gov'ner's hand,
And one's been in the pen.
Crooked legs define the bronc hands,
Cropped-off thumbs the dally men.
Their spring-toothed necks are throttled up
In silky black wild rags.
Their faces scored like flower stamps
On well-worn saddle bags.
They've come early to the funeral home,
Yet don't want to go inside.
There's no comfort in a breathless room
Or words of "eventide."
They somehow share a secret bond
As each one recollects:
Together.     Separate.     Silently.
Each pays his last respects.

You'll hear no keening to the vaulted skies,
But the good hands know when a good hand dies.

# THE TORCH IS PASSED

The branding irons are burning up.
The cutter's hand is dry.
The rasslers eye their pardners,
The ground, or search the sky.
The heeler is invisible
To the branding crew.
He's having hell.  His rope won't fit.
His loop is overdue.
You bet, they're all observing
Each futile, frantic try
The roper is delivering
From the corner of each eye.
The pressure builds.  The tension mounts
Til it's beyond belief.
Attention's shifting to the boss.
Will he call in his relief—
Tell someone else to catch his mount
And "…mebbe ketch a few?"
Embarrassing the heeler
In front of all the crew?
Then, "You savvy what's yer problem?"
Hollers out the boss.
"The reason that your loop won't fit
Is you gotta fight yer hoss.
Seen lotsa fellers do it, so
I guess it oughta work.
Spur that ol' pony's belly
'N give his head a jerk!"
He laughs, and all the hands join in.
The heeler's laughing too.
Fight his horse was what the roper
Was just about to do.
The pressure's off.  The cowboy
Builds a loop and makes it fit.
The cowboss recollects the time
That he was saved by wit:
When he was just a pistol.
Josh McCuistion was the boss.

And old Josh hollered out, "Now, kid,
Ya gotta fight yer hoss!"

The torch is passed! The past recalled.
The culture has been blessed.
The "medicine" has been renewed
Things are piva* in the West.

*Cheyenne word for "good"

# SNUFFY AND SODIE
# AND THE COWBOY CODE

"Now I ain't scared a' grizzly bears,"
    old Snuffy says one day,
"'N wolverines 'n catamounts
    to me is pure child's play.
Them trantulas and scorpions?
    I'll prance around 'em bold!
But partner, them dang rattlesnakes,
    they make my blood run cold.
I lariats my bed each night.
    My boots is tall bullhide.
I don't like bein' on the ground,
    shoot yes! That's why I ride.
Despite these nifty safety steps,
    I knows that I'll git bit.
I cogitates on remedies
    to use if I git hit.
My old Case knife is razor sharp
    to slash acrost each hole
Where that bugger's fangs went,
    still, it chills me to the soul
To plan self-mutilation,
    although it's necessary.
'N suckin' that there pizen out
    to me is awful scary.
I reckon I could do it, if
    my life was on the line.
'Cause I 'member when that critter bit
    my hoss, Sweet Adeline.
Now that pony was a kicker
    of that there's paltry doubt.
No man on earth could suck his leg
    to git the pizen out.
So his eyes they glassied over
    'n sweat jist drenched his hide.
He shuddered, then he staggered,
    'n I stood there as he died.

Sometimes I lays awake at night
    a-ponderin' on this.
'N I gits to speculatin'
    on this hypothesis:
Say now, Sodie, jist fer instance,
    we're out hossback some day,
'N old Cookie's beans has grabbed me
    in a most emphatic way.
Now I got no time to tarry,
    no sir! I'm in a rush.
But propriety it dictates
    that I got to find some brush.
Well, I gits there, but jist barely.
    There's no time to scout around.
And say—in this brush's a viper
    all coiled up on the ground.
Now I don't see him, but he sees me
    'n he feels crowded some,
So he calculates trajectory
    'n bites me on the bum.
So here I am all wounded
    but I knows what must be done,
So fishin' out my sharp Case knife,
    I carves X's on my bun.
But this I do by braille, you see,
    I'm operatin' blind,
As I carves out love and kisses
    all over my behind.
But I cain't suck the pizen out
    'cause folks ain't built for that.
Then I thinks about you, Sodie,
    'n I yells 'n waves my hat.
So you rides up, 'n I tells you
    the awful fix I'm in.
I'm checkin' all my bets to you.
    Jist you can save my skin.
My eyes is glazin' over now.
    My sun is sinkin' fast.
I'm remorseful of my sin-filled life;
    regret my pintoed past.

This nightmare here's well-water clear
    I pitcher in my mind.
I'm dyin' there. The question is,
    now, Sodie, could you find
It in yer heart to help a pal
    whose friendship is devout
'N save my life by suckin' all
    that rattler's pizen out?
'Cause the Cowboy Code, it tells
    the obligations of a friend.
It says, I quote, 'A pal must be
    faithful to the end.'"
Well, Sodie rolled and lit a smoke
    and said, "Yore right about
The Cowboy Code, but it don't
    cover suckin' pizen out.
That 'faithful to the end,' you quote
    I'd say is misdefined.
It dang sure don't require of me
    to tend to yore behind.
If you git bit, I'll fan yer face
    'n help the time pass by.
I'll speak soft words, but pardner,
    yore damn sure gonna die!"

# A SALUTE TO THE COWBOY ARTISTS

Cowboys learned how to ride from their daddies
On some wore-out gentle ranch hoss.
Cowboys learned how to cry from their mamas,
Or a rough-hewn old rawhide range boss.

The Code of the West came from movies.
John Wayne taught the saunterin' walk.
"Smile, when you call me that, stranger."
Owen Wister taught cowboys to talk.

Kindly whores and country school teachers
Gave lessons on love and on sex.
Cow punchers got safety instructions
From numerous horse and cow wrecks.

But who taught us "Laugh Kills Lonesome"?
Or be ready when "Horses Talk War..."?
It wasn't Zane Grey (though we read him);
And it sure wasn't Louis L'Amour.

But we learned to appreciate sunsets
And the beauty of unspoiled range.
And maybe we learned—call it tolerance—
For culture that at first seemed strange.

We learned hist'ry from calendar pictures.
Yes, we learned how to act and to dress,
For the values, the gear and the costumes
Seeped from canvas to subconsciousness.

Now, ev'ry cowboy that loves this old West
Has a trace of oil paint in his veins.
When the last cowboy's bones are paved over
Your record'll be all that remains

In bronze and painted on canvas,
So that "civilization" can say,
"This was the life of the cowboy.
He sure gave her hell in his day."

So here's thanks from your friends, Cowboy Artists,
We used your talents as a matter of course
As you captured forever, an era
Of the West and a man and a horse.

# GIVE US A SONG, IAN TYSON

Write me a tune, Ian Tyson,
With a beat sort of easy and slow
That will flow down each valley and canyon
From Alberta to Old Mexico.
Make it sound like the wind in the pine trees
Or the plains muffled deep in the snow.
Yes, please, write me a tune, Ian Tyson,
Like an old one the cowboys all know.

Write down some words, Ian Tyson,
Words that put a sad tear in my eye.
Words that speak of the unspoken yearning
That I have for the old days gone by.
Tell again of our shame, or our glory,
With a shout, or perhaps with a sigh.
Won't you write down some words, Ian Tyson,
Of the West, 'neath a big open sky.

Sing me your song, Ian Tyson,
Would you sing your song only for me?
Let the ripples of music transport me
Like the waves carry ships on the sea.
Make me fight, or just languidly listen.
Sing of strife, or of sweet harmony.
But please sing me your song, Ian Tyson,
Sing it softly, and easy and free.

Teach us your song, Ian Tyson,
So the cowboys can all sing along.
And forgive when we stumble and mumble
Or when we get the verses all wrong.
It's your fate to be placed as the hero
Of a bowlegged buckaroo throng.
So we'll borrow your song, Ian Tyson,
And then call it our own cowboy song.

They'll steal your song, Ian Tyson,
Steal the song that the cowboys love well.
And they'll change both the beat and the lyrics
Then they'll merchandise it with hard sell.

Let the Nashvillains ride plastic ponies
Round and round on their fake carousel.
Yet your song will remain on the ranches
Of the West where the true cowboys dwell.

Thanks for your song, Ian Tyson,
For the ballad that crept from your pen.
Out here into our hearts in the heartland
To the home of the true saddlemen.
For we're weary tonight of the strident
Of the tedious rock regimen.
So, please sing one more time, Ian Tyson,
Your song.  Yes, sing it again.

# VEGETABLE CULTIVATION

Our luck in growin' vegetables
Is dang bad, to say the least.
We're conspired against by climate
'N every kind of bug and beast.

We've planted seeds 'n watered;
Hoed until we got a sweeny.
But our cupboard's like Ms. Hubbard's
We can't even grow zucchini!

If horticulture is your short suit,
Well, pardner, here's a clue:
Don't cultivate no garden
Just cultivate some folks that do.

# THE YELLOWSTONE

Millions of buffalo curried her flanks
    as she shed winter's ice in the spring.
In the smoke of ten thousand campfires
    she heard drum beats and war dances ring.
On the crest of her bosom, she sped Captain Clark
    and Sacajawea as well.
She bisected prairie, the plains and the mountains
    from her birthplace in "John Colter's Hell."
To the trav'ler she whispered, "Come follow me,"
    with a wink and a toss of her head.
She tempted the trapper, gold miner and gambler
    to lie down by her sinuous bed.
"Safe passage," she murmured provocatively.
    "Safe passage and riches as well."
She smiled as the thread of Custer's blue line
    followed her trails and then fell.
She carved out the grade for the railroads;
    Took settlers to their new home;
Watered their stock, watered the fields,
    and let them grow crops on her loam.
Her banks were the goal of the trail herds.
    Her grass was the prize that they sought.
'Till the blizzards of 'eighty-six and seven
    nearly killed off the whole lot.
"Don't boss her, don't cross her." Let her run free,
    and damn you don't dam her at all.
She's a wild old girl, let her looks not deceive you…
    But we love her in spite of it all.

# HOWDY, MR. HUNTER

Well, howdy, Mr. Hunter, and welcome to our place.
Though I don't recall your name, or recognize your face.
I recollect your good dog there, the one a-waterin' the flowers,
The one that nailed our hens last year. We must a' spent ten hours
On butcherin' the remnants that Old Bowser left behind.
What's that you say? He's been to school a-learnin' how to mind?
Yes, it's been about a year now since we had that prairie fire.
Oh, you was huntin' here that day? It came back. The grass is higher
Than it was before it burned. Yep, we sure could a' used that hay
That went up in smoke. Ain't no idee what started it that day.
Oh! You're the one reported it? You're the one that saw the flames?
I never knowed who called it in. They never left no names.
What's that sprayer for, you ask me? It's for killin' noxious weeds.
Don't know where them buggers come from. I ain't got no leads.
Prob'ly off'n pickup mudflaps like you got there on your rig
Where some little seeds are hidin' and can grow to problems big.
You say alimony and child support give a man real grief,
And you're runnin' outa wild meat and can't afford no beef.
No, I don't want no beer, nor a gouge of stronger stuff.
But thanks for the offer. You say yer outa snuff?
I got a spare can in the house. No, I ain't got no smokes.
No, I don't believe I've heard the latest rancher jokes.
Well, have yerself a good hunt. Let me know how well you done.
Better gather up Old Bowser. Looks like he's been havin' fun.
Yah, I think thems chicken feathers caught there on his tongue.
Looks like another bunch of hens' funeral knell's been rung.
Well, to tell the truth I kinda dread all these huntin' seasons.
Why you ask? Oh, I don't know, I guess I got my reasons.

# MALCOLM AND THE STRANGLERS

I'm a fair, upstanding citizen,
    honest, trustingly true-blue,
But one time in my secret past,
    I joined a vigilante crew.

We had trailed a herd to Colstrip
    where the N.P. had a yard
And punched 'em into rail cars.
    It was hot and we'd worked hard.
My mother and Aunt Alice
    had fixed a scrumptious lunch
That the hands dispatched with relish
    after loading up the bunch.
My dad (or Uncle Evan) said,
    "Boys, lead our horses home.
We're hot 'n tired 'n sweaty;
    our backsides crave the foam
Of Chevrolet car seats, besides
    we'd be plumb insane
Not to post the buyer's check
    for the steers there on the train."
So, Duke took the reins of Peanuts
    and I led my dad's horse, Star.
We all hit the road for home,
    it wasn't all that far.
So as we're trotting homeward,
    right down the county road,
A car with California plates
    scatters gravel as it slowed
To a sliding stop amongst us
    and this family scrambles out.
They starts to snappin' pictures
    'n quizzin' Mac what we're about.
Though Malcolm's long suit's bullshit
    (plus an artful type of braggin'),
He deals 'em straight til they inquire
    on the empty mounts we're draggin'.
"We just caught and hung two rustlers,
    t'other side of that divide,

and we're fetchin' to their widows
    these two broncs they usta ride."
"You kids get in the car right now!"
    the woman volunteers.
"These men are killers! Don't look at them!
    And cover up your ears!"
The man backs up a step or two.
    "Is that legal?" he inquires.
"Far as I know," Mac says, and grins.
    "That's what the law requires."
"Are you lawmen then?" the dude asks Mac,
    as his knees begin to rattle.
"We're vigilantes," Malcolm says,
    " 'N them bastards stole some cattle."
"Could I take some camera pictures
    Of those rustlers in their tree?"
"Hell, they won't care," says Malcolm,
    "and it's sure Jake with me."

Next week, in rolls a deputy
    whose demeanor's sorta tense,
With a tale about two murders;
    says he's seekin' evidence.
Well, Malcolm, he confesses,
    concludin' California folks
Ain't got no sense of humor
    when it comes to cowboy jokes.
But somewhere out in California
    there's photographic dossiers
Of Malcolm and us Stranglers
    in our vigilante days.

# CHARLES FINLEY PARKINS

The coroner come callin'
    to the Parkins' place last week.
He loaded Charlie Finley up
    and hauled him down the creek.

Some folks thought Fin was loco,
    sorta cross-wired in the head,
But me, I kinda liked him
    and now that he is dead
I get to thinkin' 'bout him.
    Was he different? To the bone.
He somehow always was a child
    even when full grown.
They say that scarlet fever
    stole away his hearing.
His ma protected little Fin
    and passed to him her fearing
Of what the world would do to him.
    From life he was withdrawn.
He was an idle pauper prince;
    both dilettante and pawn.
He never did a lick of work
    (Well, maybe just some trifle);
Mostly slipped around the countryside
    with a rimfire rifle.
The butt of mean and nasty jokes
    was all the note he got.
It beat invisibility, I guess,
    but not a lot.
He never rode or drove a car
    or had a lady friend
Or smoked or drank or swore.
    Fin was saintly to the end.
Yet he never had religion,
    though he never raised no hell.
And when he died the neighbors said,
    "It's prob'ly just as well,

He had a long and easy life.
    It was time for him to go."
It seems to me that old Fin died
    some eighty years ago.

But…

The coroner come callin'
    to the Parkins' place last week
And loaded Charlie Finley up,
    and hauled him down the creek.

# APPLIED GENESIS

*...And God said unto man: "Be fruitful, and multiply, and replenish the earth, and subdue it, and have dominion over the fish of the sea, and over the fowl of the air, and over every living thing that moveth upon the earth." Genesis 1:28*

"I'm hereby designating you
    to serve as my straw boss."
God said, "You're on my payroll,
    so get to work now, Hoss.
You whip them critters into shape.
    Make 'em do whate'er you bid.
Just point 'em where you wanta go.
    Let your ego shape their id."

But a coyote's independent.
    He just don't seem inclined
To stand no domination.
    And them skunks? They never mind.
It aught to be plumb easy
    to forbid a hoss to buck.
Though I've choked the horn right prayerful
    I ain't had a lotta luck.
'N I been bit 'n struck 'n kicked
    more times 'n I can count
By hosses, so my bossin' don't
    seem so paramount.
There's staphs and streptococci
    (all them doobies you can't see)
That I can't keep throwed in a herd.
    They pay no mind to me.

Them lice 'n grubs 'n horn flies
    rattlesnakes and prairie dogs
Are what you'd call free spirits.
    They ignore my monologs.
"I don't mean to sound important,"
    I told this longhorn steer,
"But I'm yer boss." He got me down
    and walked off half my ear.

"Let's get this straight," I told this hen,
    "I'm boss here! Understand?
Them eggs is mine! Get off 'em,"
    and she pecked me on the hand.
I'm right proud of my position
    and this awesome job I hold.
But all them beasts 'n fish 'n fowl
    musta not been told
I'm s'posed to ramrod all them beasts
    on land, in air and sea.
But the earth and all her critters
    has got dominion over me.

# NATIONAL PARK

One year with haying over, when we wasn't fighting water,
I gather up the family, sayin', "Folks I think we aughter
Take a short vacation.  Fly off like a meaderlark
We'll relax some like civilians in a scenic Nashnul Park."
So we pack half the stuff we own in our flap-fendered car
And hit the trail for mountains that beckon from afar.
Well, we gets there in a day or so, with a minimum of fuss,
When we gets there, half the world's there too.  In line ahead of us.
'Course all our bedrolls are to home.  Ain't no place for us to stay.
The Ranger says the bears'd git us if we slept out anyway.
So we retreat, again' the grain, halfway home to some bed ground.
And contrary to all instincts, next morning turn around
And take another run.  This time we're lead wolves in the pack.
The drag is challenging us leaders and there ain't no turnin' back!
Well there's hoards of humans waitin' at every scenic spot
And we can't get outa traffic though our radiator's hot.
We seen new sights like sun bounced off'n lines of cars
     plumb blinding
And heard the eerie mating call of 'lectric cameras winding.
Heard languages from places a damn long ways from here.
Saw license plates from states that I've forgot for forty year.
And git ups?  Lord a mighty! on every shape and size of bod.
While me, wearin' what I always wear, they eye me like I'm odd!
They got words writ on their T-shirts that I know's again' the law,
That I read from 'neath my hat brim, hopin' no one seen I saw.
Oh, we saw rocks 'n trees and streams.  We seen some waterfall.
But mostly we seen humans.  Watched 'em mill 'n paw 'n bawl.
We straggled home crowd-foundered from our Park experience.
Plumb wore out like we'd branded calves, or built a mile a' fence.
You can bet your last calf check any rock pile that is steep'll
(And is called some kind of Park'll) be overrun with people.
So when we see them pretty pictures of them Parks and yearn
     to roam,
We think about them millin' herds and stay the hell to home.

# CUSTER COUNTRY

This is a land of grass and pine,
of ash and cottonwood
That the natives of the region call
"piva," "bot sots" and "good."
It's the Yellowstone and Yellowtail
yellow sandstone soaring high;
And cattle and coal and history
beneath an azure sky.
The land of the Crow and Cheyenne, too;
the land that Custer trod.
It's a land of subtle beauty
deep-rooted in prairie sod.

# TEN THOUSAND PLACES

Ten thousand places in The West
Where Nature reigned and Nature blessed
Her beasts.  There they fed and rested
For generations uncontested
By hostile humans' holy war
And man was just a visitor.
But Nature's place was so serene,
There in the forest, by the stream,
That man decided he would share
His taming with the wildness there.
He thought "The wild is cruel, chaotic,
My taming will be symbiotic."
He yearned to flee the teaming city,
Loathing it with fear and pity.
You know the rest before it's said,
Man brought with him what he fled,
To ten thousand havens in The West.
Man and Nature both oppressed,
In ten thousand places in The West.

# LITTLE THINGS

I've laid for hours upon my back
Just looking at the sky,
At clouds, or if the sky was clear,
The motes within my eye.
D'ja ever spend an hour or more
Just staring at the crick?
Or a scarab roll a ball of dung?
Or ants rasslin' with a stick?
Or, on a cloudy, windy day,
See a windmill seem to fall?
Or stop stock still with neck hairs raised
By a plaintive coyote call?
Swallows slice their swaths across
The sky like scimitars.
I'm humbled by the intricate
Snowflakes' prismic stars.
I've laughed as stove-up killdeer
Go a-scrabblin' 'cross a draw.
I've seen cedar trees explode in flames
As I'm consumed with awe.
Arms crossed and leaning forward
Weight on the saddle horn,
I'm a fascinated crowd of one;
A calf is being born.

The measure of your intellect,
The learn-ed people say,
Are the things that fascinate us.
They're a mental exposé.
You got to be dang careful
If you want to be thought smart,
And keep sorta confidential
Little things that's in your heart.

# PUT THAT BACK...HOEDOWN

*Start tapping your foot in 4/4 time and read this as if you're calling a square dance.*

Supercolliders, M H D,
    and coal-fired powerplants.
The fiddles croon; sweet is the tune.
    Now everybody dance.
For it's jobs, growth and money,
    and a song the band can play;
We'll revel through the midnight hours
    until the break of day.
Now balance with your partner
    and the gal across the hall,
For Alamand's left the cowboy life
    and he's gonna have a ball.
Promenade all to the Union Hall.
    Get hand-stamped there for life.
Sashay out with benefits for you,
    your kids and wife.
Right hand across to the MX pad,
    Tell Ivan, "Howdy-do."
Left hand back with lead gloves on
    and, "General, how are you?"
Shimmy down in a Texas Star,
    with a chain saw in your hand,
And clear-cut trees two centuries old
    to McCulloch's Ragtime Band.
Hum, hum, uranium,
    Oh hear them Geigers rattle.
This beats to hell, any-old-day,
    them days with longhorn cattle.
Buy a modern box lunch. Pay a bunch
    for a Hostess Twinkie, pard.
Promenade with Gatorade,
    and puke out in the yard.
Now, do-si-do a Case backhoe
    for another septic tank.
And two-step to your Harley, too,
    and climb a spoil bank.

Put yer little foot down. Don't be slow.
    Hear them hydraulics whine.
Another day. The pay ain't hay
    in the mother-lovin' mine.
Them power lines hum at all times
    from here down to L.A.
Turkey in the straw.  Change that law
    to make them hummers pay.
Pay the gent 30 percent.
    Too much? We'll cut her down
To an itty bitty pittance,
    or they'll close down my hometown.
Town and country get along,
    or we'll condemn your ranch,
'Cause meat it comes from IGA.
    Now everybody dance.
Dance around the outside.
    Boil that cabbage down.
Wheat and cows and sheep don't pay?
    Then ship yer kids to town.
We'll pay them dough, boy, dough, boy, dough.
    And you can sell the farm.
Or put it in the CRP;
    It won't do any harm.
Harmonee is good for me
    and you and her and him.
Chicken in the bread pan
    pickin' out dough and palladium,
Platinum and chromate ore,
    Watch out!…Another truck!
Lucky thing we come yer way,
    Oh, lucky Lady Luck!
Oh! Looky here the old coon dog
    has done laid down and died.
They're mining copper once again
    across that big divide.
Divide and conquer. Left and right,
    split right down the middle.
Cotton-eyed Joe and do-si-do.
    Now let's hear that fiddle.

Fiddle again with big BN
 and they won't haul yer grain.
Massa's on the cold cold ground;
 I'm bucked off in the rain.
Reinin' left. Reinin' right,
 on my reinin' hoss;
Hired hand up and quit today.
 Now who'll be my boss?
Circle two-step. Circle wagons.
 Who's the Circle jerk?
Minors packin' fake I.D.'s.
 Miners outa work.
Workin' on the railroad
 all the live-long day.
Skin the Cat. Dog the steer.
 Take Chapter Twelve today.
It's polka dot in the old oil spot
 as we poke that drill bit down.
Varsouvian on the old hardpan;
 then hoedown down downtown.
Chicken Reel 'n how ya feel
 as we rip across the West?
Turkey Trot in the new mall lot
 with the gal you love the best.
Let's all join hands and Circle West,
 and let the moon shine in.
Let down yer hair and rip and tear,
 destruction ain't no sin.
Now Home Sweet Home to the mobyle home
 (a 'sixty-nine New Moon).
Crank up the Ford. Don't be bored,
 just hum a cowboy tune.
Thank the boys with 'lectric toys
 that played the country dance.
Though there's damn little Country left,
 pay your money, take yer chance.
The Country Dance ain't got no chance
 if Mother Earth's a whore.
Heel and toe and away we go.
 Goin'…Gone.
  There ain't no more.

# CALL ANYTIME

Old school pals in California call up at 3 am
And ask me, "Guess who this is?" or do I remember them?
Calf buyers, tractor dealers dial my number just past dawn.
Do I want to buy Farm Journal?  Need house siding?  Greener lawn?
How about some health insurance?  Do I need a hired hand?
The surveyors for the power line need access to my land.
From Morpheus' arms they jerk me.  I stumble to the phone
I stub a toe, step on the cat but stifle back a moan
As they ask me, "Did I wake you?" I lie and tell 'em, "Nope."
Though my brain cells need a timing light; my mouth a shot of Scope.
I won't admit to sleeping.  I reject the thought with dread.
It violates the Cowboy Code being caught asleep, in bed.
I'll play my role with flannel mouth, with brain fuzzed to the hilt.
So call me at ungodly hours and I'll deal with the guilt.

# THE LIVESTOCK LEADER

He's the most successful rancher maybe, in the whole dang state.
He's a fixture, riding point, on livestock boards.
As public speaker, public figure, everyone agrees he's great.
He's hung a wall with bronze and oak awards

And pictures, shakin' hands with grinnin' folks in ties and suits,
All autographed; certificates, hung there row on row.
But still he's sorta humble; his own horn he never toots.
Like ever'body says, "He's a bunch more go than blow."

He talks to all them congressmen in Washington, D.C.
Once he led some delegation clear the hell to Rome.
Writes guest columns in the paper, 'n I guess he's on TV.
Always reppin' for us ones that stays at home.

Him I'd call a top-notch neighbor, though his fences ain't the best,
But if he's home he'll always lend a helping hand.
Oh, there's some who say he's snooty, stuck up, and all the rest.
But some of that is jealousy and some don't understand

That he works for all us part-time packin' speeches in his 'case.
But most a' them just grumble and deny it.
Wonder if they heard the news—the bank foreclosed his place—
And are wonderin', like me, on who'll buy it.

# RACHEL

Every neighborhood has got one,
    An infernal busybody,
Whose spirit is unflagging,
    Whose labor's never shoddy.

They ooze around their home range
    Scratchin' dirt to fill their craws.
Nothing's safe from their inspection
    As they search for human flaws.

Then they publicize their findings
    To anyone who'll listen,
With knowing nods and subtle winks
    Their whispering lips a-glisten.

Each natural death's suspicious.
    Every pregnancy's suspect.
Every daughter is a harlot.
    Each son, a derelect.

Every wife has secret lovers.
    Each husband is a lout.
The tangled webs of intrigue
    Go snaking all about.

Yes, our Rachel is a dandy
    As far as gossips go.
But I still talk to Rachel…
    Every month or so.

I agree that she's outrageous.
    Ain't one thing she says is true.
But it's nice to get some news
    Of the neighbors…and of you.

# DEFINITIONS OF POOR

We was dirt-poor in the thirties and forties,
Though I didn't know it back then,
'Cause it seemed we was rich when we went to the store
In town, every now and again.
We'd buy sugar and flour in hunderd-pound sacks.
Plain ones, not calico-dyed.
(Them calico prints was a dead give-away.
Mom sewed white ones. She had her pride.)
We'd buy oatmeal in Quaker Oat tom-toms
That musta been *this* big around,
Hills Brothers, Yeller boxes of soda,
Nuts in a sack by the pound.
And Dad'd get four pairs a' stiff overalls.
Mom'd get wicks for the lamps,
And some mantles for the one in the front room,
And clothespins with fancy wire clamps.
We'd get kerosene, bluing and vinegar,
And salt (with that girl in the rain),
Lime and rivets, a keg of staples, pine tar,
Stoveblack, and a length of tug chain.
The girls'd each get a hair ribbon apiece.
And Dad'd get Mom a new comb.
My prize was a bottle of or'nge Knee Hi
That I'd sip on, half the way home.
Just after he'd got his caddy of Durham,
Dad'd ask, "Charge it till fall?"
"You bet," that old storekeeper answers. "Now don't
Break down the scales in St. Paul."
Did I say we was poor? I think of them years
Way back there in my memory.
But a poor cow was hungry, so we wasn't poor.
At least that's what Dad said to me.
He said, "Sick cows is poor, while we're healthy;
And cows can get poor in a storm.
But we got a house and a stove and wood pile,
And hunderds of ways to keep warm."
"What's rich then?" I asks him. He says, "It means fat."
Then I asks him, "Ain't we sorta lean?"

"No, we're right in the middle between fat and poor.
Yep, right smack-dab there in-between!"
Of course Dad was playin' semantical games;
And foolin' with me. He'd confess.
But I think he was right. We was there in the middle
Between "poor" and "fat"…more or less.

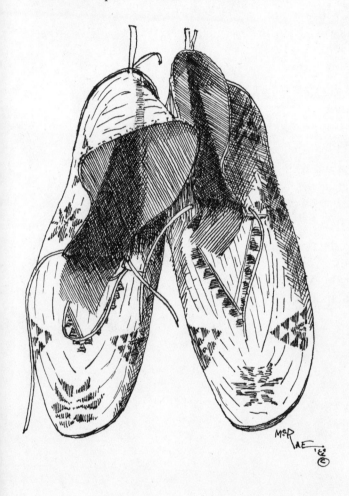

# PAX VOBISCUM

My hired hand quit the other day
Greener fields to graze.
He's packed and gone. His saddle rack
Is vacant to my gaze.

His house filled just with memories;
My footsteps echo now.
His string of horses idle stand.
They miss him too somehow.

No longer does his dog's clear bark
Announce our company.
No peal of laughter from his kids
Now breaks my reverie.

I see the country that we rode,
The calf we pulled at dawn,
The coffee pot whose brew we shared,
His quiet empty lawn.

A snoose can now reflects my stare,
As empty as my heart.
May peace be with you, Mike, my friend,
Though we be miles apart.

# SHOPPING

Dang near every Tuesday I go and watch the cattle sell
Down at the local sale barn.  I sit with Buster Fell.
Me and Buster, we go way back.  Since kids, well, we been friends.
Buster 'n me keeps up on things; politics 'n cattle trends.
We never bid on cattle.  Don't need nothin', him or me.
Then we eat a bite at Gert's Cafe; Maybe drink a tall ice tea.
I 'most always eats The Special.  Buster has the chicken fried.
We talk about the high school teams, good horses and who died.
Now lately, Clara, she's the wife, she wants to go with me.
Says she wants to do some shopping with Buster's Anna Lee.
"Whatcha need?  I'll get it."  First time out I volunteer.
"I just want to do some shopping," she says as if she didn't hear.
"For what?  I said I'd buy it.  Save you a trip to town."
"Buy what?" she says.  "Buy what you need," I says 'n sorta frown.
'Fore I knows that there's a problem, it's Katie-bar-the-door.
We pawed up dirt 'n rattled horns for an hour or maybe more.
I ask her nice, "What's eatin' you?"  Her control's about to fail.
"It's you and Buster, Gert's Cafe; and the stupid auction sale."
I tells her, "Hon, that's business.  You surely savvy that.
I gotta stay on top of things; know where the market's at."
"Do you buy anything?" she says.  "Just supper," I replied.
"It's just like shopping then," she says.  'N I'm plumb mystified.

We patched things up.  We hugged.  She cried.  But I ain't got a clue
Of what it is we fought about, but once a week we two
Meet Buster and his missus in the sale barn parking lot.
The women they go into town, but by evening they ain't bought
No more'n me 'n Buster has, 'cept for groceries and stuff,
But they seem to have a high old time, which I guess is fair enough.
We all four eats at Gert's Cafe, talk of weddings, showers and drought,
But I ain't got them women 'n their shopping figgered out.

# THE GREAT MONTANA CENTENNIAL
# CATTLE DRIVE
## THE DUDES

The first day out we worked the herd as they bounced and
    jostled by:
"Sick pen." "Cull cut." We judged each dude with a flinty
    practiced eye.
They had saddlebags of Naugahyde, canteens to wet burned lips,
Enough canvas in their dusters for a thousand sailing ships.
"What the hell we doing at this world's third dumbest event?
These gunsels sure can't sit a horse or pitch a roundup tent."
"The only thing I come to see is dudes in classic wrecks.
At this perverse, reverse rodeo it's the geeks who risk their necks."
"Seen the one with plastic stirrups? The trottin' la-la with no bra?
Tonight their knees'll be raw cube steak, 'n their gizzards
    faw-dee-graw!"
"I hear they got a sheep-decked trailer, with feather beds inside,
To haul them suckers to the airport when they limp out and quit
    the ride."
It's not that cowfolks got a mean streak a-festering inside.
But this was sorta our deal. This Centennial Cattle Ride.
Oh, they could watch us from the highway as we rode by
    straight and tall,
But it wasn't right to ride with us. Naw, that weren't right a-tall.

Two days later we're surprised some that them dudes is still along
At the fringes of the campfires, hearin' poems or cowboy song,
So they were tolerated, long as they stayed in their place.
But we never really talked to them, eye to eye, or face to face.
Oh, sure, we'd give advice to them; Or tell 'em how it's done
If they busted out and asked real nice. I pulled a cinch fer one
To keep her saddle top side, maybe save a boogered horse.
I never did it for the dude but she never knowed of course.
Once a greenhorn from New Jersey helped pack water to our camp.
When I give him my old wild rag, I swear to God his eyes
    got damp.
One night a lawyer from Chicago grazed up to our campfire ring
With a head plumb full of cowboy songs. Good Lord, that gal
    could sing!

Then a feller with a mouth harp dressed in Hollywood attire
'N a picker from Virginia drifted by to share the fire.
For a while, well, they were equals with the jaded cowboy throngs.
Of course later we recovered from the magic of their songs.
The farmers from Wisconsin who hiked the whole dang way.
We never thought they'd walk it as we passed 'em ever' day.
"Wanta hitchhike in our wagon?  You're welcome to, you bet."
They thanked us for the offer saying, "We're not quitting yet."
Could it be we'd misjudged them dudes?  Was there real sand in
     their craw?
How could they hang and rattle when their prime cuts was
     plumb raw?

So the evolution of opinion in each hand about "The Dude"
I guess you'd say transmogrified so that our attitude
(And maybe theirs) had changed until the images had blurred.
And the wall that separated us slowly seemed absurd.
See, us riders growed together like we never woulda guessed.
Instead of driftin' off in sep'rate cuts we somehow coalesced.
All the dif'rences between us seemed to settle in the dust.
The unspoken word on wind-chapped lips was "Billings Heights
     or Bust."
It wasn't "them" and "us" no more.  It was "Can I help you, pard?"
And "We'll all ride straight and tall and proud right down that
     boulevard."
The hikers and the floppers and us hands that poked the fun
All swallered back them tears of pride and, damn it, we was one!
The critics claim the whole dang deal was B.S.  Were they right?
"A waste of time?"  "High cowboy kitch?"  "A high camp cow
     camp blight?"
The Cattle Drive?  Magnificent!  Each critic must admit.
When cowfolks rode old Cowboy Pride.  And dudes showed
     cowboy grit.

# DOCK GROOM

I see a yeller Studebaker
    easin' down the crick.
Ol Dock, 'n 'Ceil, 'n Ruthie
    has got some plums to pick.
I bet Ruthie's grinnin' in the back,
    while up front is Dock and 'Ceil.
You'd think they was a family,
    but naw, that ain't the deal.
Carl Whitaker is Ruthie's dad,
    and 'Ceil's Carl's wife.
And Carl is prob'ly Dock's best friend,
    has been all his life.
But mostly Carl he stays to home
    a-putterin' aroun'
While Dock 'n 'Ceil 'n Ruthie
    goes motorin' to town.
Pore Ruthie's never been all there
    since back when she was foaled,
An' she must be, well let's see now,
    some forty-odd years old.
It's nice of Dock to haul them 'round
    and Carl don't cause no strife.
It prob'ly tickles old Dock some
    when folks think 'Ceil's his wife.
Carl and Dock is trappers, see,
    been partners now for years.
They've caught a thousand coyotes,
    I suppose, in their careers.
I reckon most the headdresses
    the Cheyennes wear was made
From eagles and from ermine,
    that they got from Dock in trade.
Dock used to do live trappin'
    but he got too old fer that.
He caught a pure white porcupine
    and hunerds of bobcat.
Dock hunts and traps the year around.
    Some folks don't think that's right.

But he's never been on welfare,
    Prides hisself on livin' light.
"There's worlds a' coyotes, kid," Dock says.
    And I reckon he should know.
Except fer Dock, his breed died out
    a hunderd years ago.
He runs his traplines nowadays
    in a Studebaker Lark.
At the signposts of gentility,
    he sniffed, and left his mark.

Dock's got a tarp and buckets
    piled in the car-top rack.
He and 'Ceil both give a wave.
    Ruthie's grinnin' there in back.

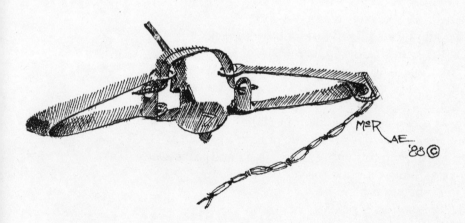

# HIRED HAND

You know, some men just look like a cowboy,
Though you'd be hard-pressed to say why.
It may be their posture, or bearing,
Or the confident look in their eye.

Since I was needing some ranch help,
I tapped into the cowboy grapevine,
Where every saloon and each bunkhouse
Can transmit, or receive, on the line.
Later on, well, in rolls this pickup
With them buckin' hoss Wyoming plates,
'N the hat that the driver was wearing
Looks like a twin of George Strait's.
There's rawhide mudflaps on the outfit
And a big gooseneck ball in the back,
A bedroll, a basket-stamped A-fork,
The gun rack's plumb festooned with tack.
On the windshield's a Quarter Horse sticker
From clear back in seventy-seven.
"Mighty nice country" 's the first words he spoke
"It sure looks to be a cow heaven.
I was down at the sale barn in Sturgis
Where I hears that yer needin' a hand,
So I drives up through Belle Fourche and Lame Deer
Maybe thinkin' to ride for yer brand.
I'm no hell of a hand now, you savvy?"
(Here he offers a pinch of his snoose.)
"There's lotsa good hands in the country
'N I'm just a sorry excuse.
But all I been's just a cowboy.
I follered a cow all my life.
I guess if I'd been more aggressive
I'd maybe still have me a wife.
I lost her 'n them cows, I guess nine years ago.
She called losin' our cows the last straw.
She called me a loser (prob'ly she's right),
And moved back with the mother-in-law.
As a hand goes, I guess I'm just av'rage,
Or maybe a notch below that.
I'm partial t'wards lady-broke horses

That couldn't buck off a man's hat.
Now some people brag on their ropin'
That can't find their way outa town.
Me?  If I can't catch 'em runnin',
I keep chargin' until they lay down.
I'd say I'm a lousy horseshoer;
'N machinery I don't cotton to.
Do I drink? Well, I ain't no abstainer
'N I like to hoist me a few."
He went on a-jokin' and jobbin'
With a humorous gleam in his eye.
Damned if I didn't right away find myself
Laughin' and likin' this guy.
I'd had it with all of them blowhards
With them buckles proclaiming them "Champ."
He could roll out his bed in the bunkhouse;
Diogenes could hang up the lamp.
Here for damn sure was the last honest man,
Who was humble—devoid of all guile.
I figured that here was a cowboy
That could do it all...with a smile.

I was led like a poddy to slaughter.
I'm amazed, 'n I bet you are, too.
The sumbitch was a liar, I tell ya,
Ev'ry word that he told me was true!

# WEEDS

The lawn is filled with dandelions
There's thistles in the hay.
Got knapweed in some pastures,
I just seen some more today.

Our rhubarb garners compliments.
(They don't know it's cocklebur.)
Fuzzies offin' milkweed
Make my vision seem to blur.

I'm the County Agent's dream come true.
He runs buses to my place.
I'm a perfect bad example,
A horticultural disgrace.

'Cause there's kochia in the sweet corn
Bind weed's chokin' the Swiss chard
And we got some bloomin' pig weed
A-bloomin' in our yard.

Ruthie's marigolds are under siege!
The iris hoisted their white flag.
We got weeds of all descriptions.
Horse, and fire, chick and rag.

But ranch management advisors
Say we each gotta find our niche.
Well!  I've got recent information
That's gonna make me rich.

From a hailed out hippie buddy
Gonna follow up his lead
And take advantage of this market.
'Cause he wants to buy some weed.

# BOX ELDERS

A box elder's a plumb sorry tree
That lays down as it grows.
It genuflects on gouty knees
To wind and wet spring snows.

Its git-up-and-go has gone and went.
It's mighty shy of spunk.
Its branches are arthritic-bent.
Its spine is weak with punk.

Poor lowly kin of cottonwood,
Of stately pine and ash.
A warty dwarf—misunderstood,
A sylvan poor white trash.

With hearts as red as heroes' blood
(Though no medals grace their breast),
Supine, their trunks defy the flood
With nonviolent protest.

The creek bank's stitched with double seam
Of box elders, slouched at ease.
Hipshot, faithful...calm work team...
Faithful country trees.

# AIN'T NO COWBOY HEAVEN

Whenever western writers write
Of the cowboy and his dismal plight,
They describe a blissful sequel waiting there at eventide.
From his hell on earth he earns reprieve,
And as compensation he's bound to receive
A perpetual promise of punchin' cows, when he crosses the
    Big Divide.
The odds on this I've give some thought,
But I ain't sure a puncher ought
To bank upon no program where he might be dealt up short.
I always learnt to shy away
From "too good to be true" deals, 'n who's to say
They'd allow them messy cows up there?  Nope, I doubt they'd
    make the sort.
As near as we come to heaven down here
Is a wilderness, and it seems plumb clear
They ain't gonna let no poopin' cows up there in paradise.
I'll see your raise 'n bump the bet
If you think Saint Pete's agonna let
Some cows or broncs or dogs up there again' the Board a'
    Health's advice.
'N them angels there—they don't partake
On biscuit, beans 'n greasy steak;
'N a cowpoke's microflora'd die on grub like honey 'n milk.
So we'd get puny 'n mebbe die.
I doubt we'd keep our bedrolls dry
Whilst sleepin through some cloudbust in a bed tent made a' silk.
If things went smooth we'd get plumb bored,
So ever' week or so The Lord,
Just to keep us happy, would create some great big wreck.
You reckon we'd get our work done
'N charge around 'n have some fun
If we couldn't use some earthy words?  Not even "dang" or "heck."
Them wing'd DVMs'd think us fools
Usin' words like "urine," "rectum" 'n "stools"
When ridin' on them sick pens at the feedlot in the sky.
No lots, y'say, on account a' smell?
So they've been banished down to Hell?

Well, where do them feedlot cowfolks go when they quinine
        up and die?
Don't seem fair they gotta go ride Lucifer's pens down there below.
They've had their share of mis'ry, I heard, so s'pose it's so.
There ain't gonna be no cards or booze.
So what'll all them buckaroos
Do for entertainment?  Race sweet chariots to and fro?
No use to race if bettin's out.
Maybe tie some hondas good an' stout
In golden cords, to rope fatted calves with loops for head 'n heel?
Never happen!  You really think
The Lord'd abide the awful shrink
Them pukin' rollin' ropers'd render off His veal?
You can hoorah me for a doubtin' Tom
I'll take yer abuse; stay cool 'n calm,
'Cause I can prove there ain't no heaven for a passed on buckaroo.
You can vilify me as a low down liar
But Heaven don't have no brandin' fire
The Devil's done cornered the market.  You know dang well
        that's true.
So:
If you wanta cowboy in the afterlife
Then gamble 'n covet 'n beat the wife
'N lie 'n cheat 'n steal 'n kill 'n cuss 'n lout 'n loot.
Bear false witness.  Fight yer hoss.
Gamble 'n lust 'n hit the sauce.
Go on and chouse them cows forever in yer asbestos union suit.

# THE LINGO OF OUR CALLIN'

Now, let's say that you had growed up
    where the cowtrails all is paved,
So's the lingo of our callin' warn't too clear.
And you really didn't savvy when a puncher up and raved
And volleyed some strange words again' yer ear.

Now then, we'd sure call their autopass
    by the name of cattleguard,
And say that somethin' wild was pretty rank,
Or honky or even ringy, but them dudes, I tell you pard,
Don't know their frog from poll, or shank from flank.

A poddy, chinks, a soogin, mill-tailed-dandy words is those,
And gaskin, goosie, gotch-eyed and quarter crack.
Lazy, hangin', runnin', slash that there hot-iron talkin' goes.
There's nibs, and cribs and game, and high, low, jack.

There's heaves and scours and spavins. Thrush and fistuloes.
Earmarks, jaw waddles, dewlaps and jingle bobs.
And there's both bagged- and mothered-up,
    both grass ropes and grass widows.
And fifteen-two,-four,-six and jack for nobs.

There's back-formed verbs like rimrocked,
    hoolihanned, and bitted-up,
Hot shotted, bummed, and cribbed, and pencil shrunk.
And there's point, and heel…and doggin'
    (which is done without a pup).
And goose-egged is the past tense of skunk.

Say you spoke of this here outfit that had jockeys and a horn,
Plus a tree.  Was rigged a seven-eights, or full.
And had swells, and skirts, and fenders. Well, just
    sure as you was born,
A lot of folks would say you're spoutin' bull.

Roman noses ain't too noble.  I'd be 'shamed of cuttin' proud.
Parrot mouths is worth, mostly, canner prices.
Cow- and sickle-hocks don't make it. Solid bays
    and browns ain't loud.
Glass- and pig-eyed mounts got different vices.

What kind of stove's a Sibley?  Ever seen a cook tent fly?
How come forelocks only equal one?
Why can't a puncher steer a cow?  What flavor's a cow pie?
Oh say?   Ain't all these riddles dandy fun?!!

We've got spades, and curbs, and half-breeds,
     snaffles, crickets in the port.
And muley is the opposite of horned.
There's cutters and ropers among cacks of every sort...
But bear traps is most generally scorned.

Well there's swaller-forks and A-forks...and forked (the adjective).
There's Pendeltons (and a California) pant.
Sundry tack; and tackaberrys (which'll pile you if they give).
And a dry cow ain't necessarily gaunt.

There's scotch hobbles and honyockers. Horse cavvy
     and calvie cows.
There's black-leg, bog spavin, gas (and frothy) bloats.
There's bosals, quirts and martingales. Cuds and cods
     and chuck (for chow).
And slicker, sheep, and rooster-skin type coats.

Savvy coulees, draws and gunions? How 'bout jigs
     and jogs and lopes?
There's pacers, single-foots, and puddin'-taters.
McCarties, fiadores and rowels.  Hair and silk manila ropes.
Hog-leg, and smoke-pole sievelators.

Well now, that's the last bull rider...'cept for
     rerides and the slack.
The fiddler just started playing "Home Sweet Home";
I'll just cast off all my dallies, shake some makin's from my sack.
I took up all the slack in this here pome.

# A COST-RETURN ANALYSIS

I gave a calf a three-way blackleg shot,
And some pen-strep, cause she didn't look so hot.
I thought some A-D-E would help a lot.
Kicked in a mineral mix, that's pretty hot.

I poured some stuff upon her back for lice
And grubs and other critters that ain't nice.
I gave her sulfa pills, on vet's advice,
And dosed her up with worm stuff, once or twice.

I tuned her up on concentrates unique.
And had her going fat, and fit, and sleek,
Aiming for a cow conditional peak…
And then she went and drownded in the creek.

# HANDY HARRY

You've known guys like Harry, so handy they're scary.
Whatever needs done, they can do it.
It's a lead pipe cinch, if you get in a pinch,
That they'll push you aside and hop to it.

It wasn't Harry's intention to create dissension;
No gauntlets did he mean to toss,
When he'd waltz right in with a shy sort of grin
And show you up, in front of the boss.

He could tie fiadors and unlock the doors
Of pickups with keys locked inside.
"Pure luck," he'd insist when the cattle we'd missed
He'd gather, whenever we'd ride.

He could rig up a pulley and understood fully
Laws of motion and how they applied.
He could rope like a pro, braid rawhide and sew
Up wirecuts few vets would have tried.

Our egos was dented.  We sulked and resented
Old Harry.  Evil notions was fizzin'.
We couldn't help mopin' and secretly hopin'
That someday old Harry'd get hizzin'.

One day found the boss and us hands at a loss
On some job and just how we should do it,
When Old Harry jumped in with a laugh and a grin
To show us all up…and he blew it.

# ME AND THE HIPPIE ON THE GREYHOUND BUS

"What sign was you born underneath?"
This hippie ast of me.
"The D Six one," I volunteered.
He shore looked strange at me.

I figgered I'd confused him some,
So, to explain, I said:
"But now I'm under Rocker Six."
But he just shook his head.

He ast me what day I was born,
And I told him real brief.
He said that my sign was a fish.
But I told him, "No it's beef."

He talked about the pad he had
(Which he shared with all his friends).
Mine's made of hair.  And he says, "Cool."
So I know he comprehends.

He brought up Boone's Farm to me,
Like it was stuff he'd drank.
I said, "Back in the thirties,
It was foreclosed by the bank."

He just plumb mothered-up to me,
And said I was shore a gas.
When he ast what my outfit growed,
And I said, "Just mostly grass."

He ast me if I smoked it,
(How he knowed, I can't assay).
But I said, "Yes, when burning trash
And the damn fire got away."

That answer must have throwed him off.
So he says, "Do you use Pot?"
I told him it twarn't his business
What facilities I got.

He wondered if I was a Head.
And I answered back, "Why shore."
Though I been behind more often,
If a man was keepin' score.

He talked about this here Roach Clip,
And how he prized it so,
But if he had his mane roached, it
Had bin a long time ago.

When he ast 'bout Speed, I told him,
"No sir, I don't use her much,
Not with the roads we got at home,
With them ruts, and rocks and such."

How 'bout Coke?  He ast me then.
I replied, "I don't partake.
For even tho I like the taste,
Cold drinks make my fillings ache."

You know 'bout LSD's? he says.
And I volunteered, "Why shore,
They used them in them landings
In the Second World War."

He said he'd never tried no Horse.
(Well now that was plain to see).
No self-respectin' cayuse would
Let him on, it seems to me.

I told him it weren't possible
For me to donate him some Bread.
"It don't keep if I carry it."
"I know what you mean," he said.

"You shore are square," he volleys up.
And I answered modestly,
"Why, it's nice of you to say so,
I shore do figure to be."

We up and went our sep'rate ways,
But I ain't seen no sweller
Kind of a guy to visit with,
Than that there hippie feller.

# BAREBACK RIDER
FOR PAUL ZARZYSKI

He used to turn his toes out; reach and jerk among the best.
He lusted for the barebacks; spurred with style.
He packed his card with pride, like a medal on his breast.
He'd stroke for eight then dismount with a smile.

Things was tough where he growed up, so he growed up tough
      as well.
His old man was just another grunting Polock at the mine.
A high school gridiron symphony enticed him for a spell
But he struck out for the West to cut new sign.

Time and place, and the hunger for a new adrenal high
All conspired to fix his focus on the bares.
Cut his saddle teeth at Kesler's; learned grit 'n guts 'n try;
Paid apprentice fees at all the local fairs.

Well, he never made no money. Hell, that's not what it's about!
There's damn few hands who spur for praise or pay.
It's the feeling that you get when the gate man turns him out
And it's you and horse and sky. Exult, or pray

That this one's finally perfect. Condemn to Hell the judges' cards.
The score that counts while shankin' one that's rank
Is the one inside your head; in the backslaps of your pards.
It's not the silver buckles or the greenbacks in the bank.

Then it's over. But, damn it, is it? Must the curtain slowly fall?
Who can say: "This one'll be, at last, my final ride.
I'm one sumbuck never quit with my back again' the wall.
I paid my dues. I got my cowboy pride!"

But it's over, and he knows it. "Hang 'em up," his mind dictates.
"There's more to life than spurrin' out a bare.
You quit your football helmet, retired the hockey skates,
And life's parading by. Go grab your share."

Though it's over, and he knows it. His heart won't go along.
There's a vacuum metered out in eight-tick spurts.
He wants to feel, just one more time, the singing rowel song.
He'll miss it, Lord, and no one knows it hurts.

He's my friend, and I can't help him.  Though I wish to hell I could.
But he don't need no crutch to walk this lonely mile.
If he had a phone, I'd call him:  tell him that I understood.
Hell, he knows that...I'll see him in a while.

# HOLIDAY SEASON

"Happy Holidays," they tell me,
"Merry Christmas to you all."
There's snow songs on the TeeVee,
And Santy's in the Mall.

The mailbox bursts with catalogs.
Our checkbook's in the red.
Rudolph's headin' up a jerkline,
Snakin' skyward with a sled.

Raise a glass in celebration
Of a bountiful New Year.
Tis the season to be jolly.
Kill a tree and give a cheer.

But the snow is deep and drifted.
We're haulin' feed and choppin' ice.
So to folks in charge of calendars,
I'll give you some advice:

You change some dates around a bit,
I'll join in—hell for leather,
But it ain't no joyous season
When you're fightin' winter weather.

# MY REQUIEM

Some leave their mark on a branded hide.
Some on the furrowed earth.
Some aspire to reproduce
Themselves in those they birth.
Some leave their marks on canvas,
Bronze or stone that will survive.
Long after their creator
No longer is alive.

Some would build an edifice,
An architectural gem,
To serve throughout the ages
As a lasting requiem.
But grant to me this final wish
When I say that last amen:
Let my mark be carried lightly
In the hearts and minds of men.

# THE COMPLEAT COWBOY

Trade my old rough-out for a flower stamp.
My rusty curb for a silver spade.
Retire the plain bronc spurs for a blued steel pair
That are fashionably inlaid.

A tasteful silver concho or two.
And a new fringed Navajo.
A hair headstall, and a horn cap made
Of silver from Mexico.

A pair of buckstitched shotguns,
Instead of my worn-out chaps.
A new silver-belly with an RCA crease,
'Stead of feed, and implement caps.

I'll never get all of that fancy tack
Even if I could.
'Cause you better be as good as you look.
And I just ain't that good.

# DIFFERENT DRUMMERS

The rumbling bridge and the barking dog
Announce coming company,
And a respite from the daily chores.
As I wait expectantly,
Hoping the coming visitor
Will stay to sleep and eat
And mutually entertain us,
With hours of talk replete.

The rumbling bridge and the barking dog
Differently affect my wife.
The unmown yard and the rumpled house
Fill her mind with strife:
"What if they stay to eat and sleep?
What can I thaw for dinner?"
Side by side expectantly we wait,
The victim…and the sinner.

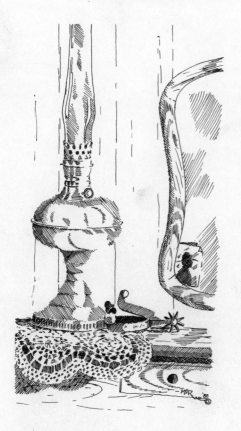

# RIDERS' BLOCK

Tonight they're trying, once again,
With pencils poised, impatient pen,
To scribe the ultimate in verse.
They write, erase; they chafe and curse
In roundup camp, in barroom smoke
To braid in rhyme the latest joke.
The quest to fill the current rage
For cowboy pomes, to mount the stage
In Elko, is their hearts' desire.
They writhe in rage beside the fire.
Each stanza's formed, in diagram,
In foreheads throbbing with iamb.
Prepared to drop each "G" in "ing."
Slick metaphors are poised to spring.
All they need's a topic, yet
Each mind is numb.  They squirm and sweat.
They quick-draw blanks.  They should be fannin'
Bull's-eyes aimed at Elder Cannon!
Why!  They could rival Badger Clark!
If mental coils produced one spark
To light this black hole, filled with doubt.
But no!  No mark, they missed him out.
To hell with humor!  Nostalgia then?
A saga of bold saddlemen?
A cutting swipe at dudes?  Or women?
Or bureaucrats?  Their minds are swimmin'.
Damn Zarzyski, Michael Logan,
Who never lack a theme or slogan
Or inspiration for a rhyme.
What's their gimmick?  Why's it I'm
Stuck here rimrocked, thinking zero,
When I could be a western hero
On Western Horseman's poet's page?
A sagebrush rhyming cowboy sage.
My powder's wet.  The well is dry.
Calliope has passed me by.

Take heart, all you rhyming pards,
The West is filled with want-to bards
Just two quarts low of inspiration,
Filled tonight with great frustration.
Horse rider's block, you're right, 's a curse,
But pardner, there's one problem worse:
It's them that's got but zilch to say
But goes and writes 'em anyway.

# SIGNS

It's not the crying V's of geese
A-flying overhead.
Nor the inconspicuous buckbrush
Suddenly, strident red.

It's not the horses hairing-up,
The creek a-turning brown.
Or the ash tree getting gussied up
In her saffron dressing gown.

It's not the blue-tinged frosty morn,
The coyote getting bolder,
The faint ache in my steel-pinned leg
Reminding me I'm older.

It's not the spring-green grasses,
Now a tannish monochrome.
I know that fall's upon us—
Our cats are coming home.

# GOOSEBERRIES

Gooseberry bushes with hostility bristle
To prickle your imprudent hands.
Their alum-sour fruit will burgle your whistle—
Assaulting your maxilla glands.

Gooseberry bushes are uncommonly common.
Few sponsors their praises will sing.
For a bit each year they gladden the land,
The first greening leaves of the spring.

# JERRY KINZEL

"Ash wood," said Jerry Kinzel.
"Ash wood is what it takes,
If you cowboys want fit vittles
From me that cooks and bakes."
Ash wood it was for the roundup stove,
For the cook's least whim was law.
And all us kids and hands and such
Viewed Jerry, the cook, with awe.

"Pitch pine's the only kinda wood
You bow-leg bastards know.
But that that's fit fer brandin' irons
Don't work to cook, you know.
It burns the crust on pie and bread,
But leaves the middle soggy.
Kinda like some folks I know
Whose mommas was a doggy."

"You think you fool me, don'tcha,
With that pile a' cottonwood.
You'll pay the price at suppertime,
When the apple pie ain't good.
And get that damn horse outa here,
Or I'll cut off yer nose—
Unless you got him potty-trained,
Or manure smells like a rose."

"Cheap damn Scotchman outfit,"
One day old Jerry said,
"The only one I ever seen
Too Scotch fer store-bought bread."
"Hell, Jerry, you don't have to bake,"
Said the boss with kindly mien.
"Oh, I don't mind," gloats Jerry,
"Kneadin' keeps my hands plumb clean."

"I don't mind all the cookin',
And movin' camp and such.
But dish washin' and dryin'
Wouldn't hurt some folks too much.
But you don't hafta help me

When the dishes all get dirty,
We'll go to usin' cow pies,
Which'll make our camp ground purty."

"Why some folks'll use more water,
Just to wash their hands,
Than is took to wash two sheepherders,
And water up their bands.
And then they dump the basin
Just outside the fly.
So don't call fer me if you bog down.
I damn sure won't reply."

Stubble-bearded and rheumy-eyed,
With bunions on his feet.
Sour and cynical his vein,
But did we ever eat!
A roll-yer-own hid toothless gums,
And gruffness hid his heart.
Both crabbiness and cookin'
He had practiced to an art.

Somewhere in an ethereal land,
Among the cumulus,
Old Jerry's cowin' cowboys with
His blusterin' cussin' fuss.
But each angelic cowpoke,
As he rolls out of his bed,
Can bet his wings and halo that
He'll damn sure be well fed!

# CLINT

He sometimes turns his horse's tail
Wrong-ways to a cow.
He still can't tie a bowline,
Though I have showed him how.

Once he took a brace and bit
And drilled it in the dirt.
He left his boots out in the rain,
And yonder lies his shirt.

He tried to take his saddle off,
Forgetting the back cinch,
And somehow kinked the cable
On my calf-pulling winch.

Once he filled my water jug
Plumb full of gasoline.
Wore a groove into my grindstone.
At school, said words obscene.

He lost a brand-new Crescent wrench.
Nicked a new hoof nipper.
Took my pinchers from their pocket,
And "fixed" my new chap zipper.

Spilled grease upon my welding rod.
Broke eggs in my felt hat.
Then in the lot at weaning time,
Sicked the dog upon a cat.

When we were corralling cattle, once,
He met us on his trike.
Scratched his name upon my saddle
With a marlinespike.

My boy has done 'er all, my friends.
He's constantly in trouble.
Yet, folks who knew me as a kid
Insist that he's my double.

Their recollection's faulty.
I dispute it with a curse.
I wasn't like him, growing up.
I was a whole lot worse.

# ON RURAL RELOCATION

"Ranch home wanted for large dog," say the ads.
And, "Cute kittens need a farm home."
"My city kid's got bad companions,
Needs hard work, and country to roam."

You'd send us all of your paranoid pets.
And the sad, frightened critters you birth.
The kids and the kittens, the rejects and dregs.
Yes, get them back to earth.

But we don't need your problem kids, cats and dogs.
Your delinquents, rejects and such.
We've got problems enough out here on the ranch.
So thanks, but no thanks very much.

# THE DEBUT

Well, now, Gillie told this story, so on its truth you can't rely,
Since them sainted sons of Erin is a bit inclined to lie.
But this is how he told it, so I'll leave it up to you.
It may be bull or blarney, then again it might be true.

Seems there was this trav'lin road show come rollin' into town
To stage a melodrama.  But one dramatist was down
With the grippe or the consumption or a case of green gomboo.
But whichever was the ailment, it laid low the ingenue.
But the part was just a smidgen (some paltry lines, I guess).
So the ramrod of the road show says, "We ain't in no big mess.
I'll just singlefoot up Main Street, and hold me an audition
To fill the vacancy in our dramatic composition."

So after he'd explained the deal to the first prospect he met,
And asked her if she'd lend a hand, she answered,
    "Yes, you bet."
The lady tried her costume, her few lines and learned the plot,
And was nonplussed to discover that she was to be shot
By the evil villainess (who fired a gun with blanks).
"No problem," says the lady. "It sounds like fun. And thanks."

Well, that same night the Lyceum hummed with expectation,
Though the "Patrons of the Arts" was mostly cowboys on
    vacation.
They'd drunk their share of Tiger Tears, so with spirits
    unrestrained,
Their two-bit entry fee insured that they'd be entertained.
With rapt anticipation they watched the plot unfold
Betwixt the noble hero and the villain, vile and cold.
Yet the one they most despised for her base shamelessness,
Was the evil villain's side-kick, the sulky villainess.
The cowpokes, silent, spellbound, watched the drama seethe
    and rage,
Until the local woman minced onto the stage.
Now, each eye that beheld her knew this woman well.
And silence fell upon the crowd as if by fun'ral knell.
A saucy French maid's uniform she wore, as on her way,
She lightly tripped across the boards with her tea service tray.

The villainess, with pistol drawn, was raging on with ire
As the local lass, unheeding, crossed the line of fire.
A shot rang out! Down went the maid! The silver tea set flew.
A shocked and silent audience's hearts went crashing too.
"What have I done?" the villainess asked rhetoric'ly.
"What have I done?" she asked again, as she prepared to flee.
One cowpoke jumped up boldly, despite the smoking gun,
And broke the dreadful silence with, "I'll tell you what you done."
Breaking with emotion, the cowboy's voice grew sad,
"You jist shot the best damn whore that this town ever had!"

# E. M. (RED) KLUVER

What sort of a man was the Red Pup, you say?
Hard, Oh Lord, he was hard.
And how did he go? Did he just slip away?
Hard, No Lord, he died hard.

And how did he live? Was he easy and free?
Hard, Oh Lord, he lived hard.
Now in the big war, did he cower and flee?
Hard, No Lord, he fought hard.

He used to ride broncs. Did he have the knack?
Hard, Oh Lord, he rode hard.
And how did he work? Did he kinda lay back?
Hard, Oh Lord, he worked hard.

What of his looks? Was he attractively made?
Hard, Oh Lord, he looked hard.
What of his values? Was he easily swayed?
Hard, No Lord, he was hard.

Not soft then, or wavering? You'd say in its stead...
Hard, Oh Lord, he was hard.
And how do you feel, now that he's dead?
Hard, Oh Lord, it's so hard.

# RODEO

Here we go, to the rodeo,
For a rousing, rollicking time.
To drink a beer, and give a cheer
For the go-round's fastest time.

Cheer the spills, and all the thrills,
Of the bucking horse, and bull.
Join the throaty roar, that beats down o'er
The arena, from bleachers full.

There's the crushing hush, the heady rush,
For a bull rider that is down.
Then comes relief, saved from grief,
He's snatched from harm by the clown.

We'll cheer the chaps, in flashing chaps,
And cheer for the critters they ride.
The girls barrel race. There time and space
Are combined and personified.

The lariats smoke, as ropers rope
At the horns, and then at the heels.
Calf horses slide, as their riders glide
To the calf, as he cartwheels.

Kids get their fill. They eat and swill
Hotdogs, and strawberry pop.
Clouds in the west give rumbling protest.
We're shocked by a lone raindrop.

Each calf's been tied. The re-rides tried.
And here comes a man with a broom.
Back home we'll go, from the rodeo,
Once the kids have hit the bathroom.

Each nose has a burn. We no longer yearn
To be a part of the rodeo clique.
It's been a thrill, but we've had our fill
Of cowboys…at least for a week.

# SOLD TO THE HIGHEST BIDDER

"Sold to the highest bidder!"
The gavel crashes down.
Another rural family
Goes shamblin' into town.

    Sold to the highest bidder,
    Their dreams go down, dirt-cheap;
    Where every dream's a nightmare
    Endured in fitful sleep.

Sold to the highest bidder
The trinkets forged with tears,
Framed pictures on the bureau
Of graduation years.

    Sold to the highest bidder.
    To town go the crocks and jars,
    Just knick-knacks now, or planters
    In condos or fern bars.

Sold to the highest bidder,
The cowbell and milk pail.
"They're chic," observes a shallow voice,
"I'll hang them on a nail."

    "Sold to the highest bidder!"
    The gavel crashes down.
    Another rural family
    Goes shamblin' into town.

# THINGS OF INTRINSIC WORTH

Remember that sandrock on Emmells Crick
Where Dad carved his name in 'thirteen?
It's been blasted down into rubble
And interred by their dragline machine.
Where Fadhls lived, at the old Milar place,
Where us kids stole melons at night?
They 'dozed it up in a funeral pyre
Then torched it.  It's gone alright.
The "C" on the hill, and the water tanks
Are now classified "reclaimed land."
They're thinking of building a golf course
Out there, so I understand.
The old Egan homestead's an ash pond
That they say is eighty feet deep.
The branding corral at the Douglas camp
Is underneath a spoil heap.
And across the crick is a tipple, now,
Where they load coal onto a train.
The Mae West Rock on Hay Coulee?
Just black-and-white snapshots remain.
There's a railroad loop and a coal storage shed
Where the bison kill site used to be.
The Guy place is gone; Ambrose's, too.
Beulah Farley's a ranch refugee.

But things are booming.  We've got this new school
That's envied across the whole state.
When folks up and ask, "How's things goin' down there?"
I grin like a fool and say, "Great!"
Great God, how we're doin'! We're rollin' in dough,
As they tear and they ravage The Earth.
And nobody knows...or nobody cares...
About things of intrinsic worth.

# TOUCHY QUESTIONS

You can ask how old I am
And how many kids I got.
But I'll get right shifty-eyed
If you ask what my calves brought.

I'll tell you of some horses
I rode, or I still got.
But the price is sorta private
On that new stud that I bought.

I'll admit to old romances,
Old friendships gone to pot,
But it just ain't yer business
Of the debts or deals I got.

I'll tell the distance into town.
…How cold it got, or hot.
But I won't even hint at
How big a place I got.

So just ask any question
I'll answer like a shot.
'Cept for the aforementioned…
Or how many cows I got.

# ROUNDUP'S OVER

I been mashin' them critters and brandin' them calves
Since the wagon pulled out, back in May.
But I rolled out my bed for the last time this year.
Work's done.  Boys, it's time now to play.

I've done ate up my share of blue brandin' smoke
And of dust and them Dutch-oven beans.
I'll just test out my rump on a civilized chair
And my charm on some honky-tonk queens.

I'll shed off some hair, shuck these horse sweaty clothes,
Rediscover hot water and soap.
The cavvie's strung out.  They know that we're goin'
To headquarters at a long lope.

Old camp cookie's flapjacks and biscuits I'll miss some;
But I won't miss his "Cowboys roll out!"
There's a clean wild rag in my war bag somewhere,
And a semi-clean shirt, no doubt.

Some smoky saloon may get half my pay.
There's sidewalks I hanker to stroll.
You'll know I've arrived when you see me show up
With my spurs—out at the town hole!

# URBAN COWBOY

Look at him there with his hat all rared back,
A purple plume peekin' over its crown.
Hair's pokin' out of his unsnapped shirt front.
On his back a desert sun's goin' down.

A turquoise leaf-shape, that sure ain't no palm,
Is inlaid on his pointy-finger ring.
One ostrich-hide boot points off toward grandma's,
Like he might *pas de bah* to a Fling.

His hair's all feathered and teased at the fringe.
A bead and bear claw doodad's on his neck.
He won't meet yore eye, but shows his profile,
Like the jack of hearts, fresh cut from a deck.

There's insects and plants like I never seen
Filigreed on his one boot top that shows.
That fierce black lion, tatooed on his arm,
Is locked in mortal combat with a rose.

I'd guess his buckle's a Packard hubcap
Holdin' a horse just a buckin' fer fair,
Whose feet's made of jade; a ruby's his eye.
It's on a belt made of wicker and hair.

Jist look at him there, a-reekin' of Brut,
Favorin' us one and all with his class.
He may be somethin', but I bet he ain't—
A mere pimple on a real cowboy's ass.

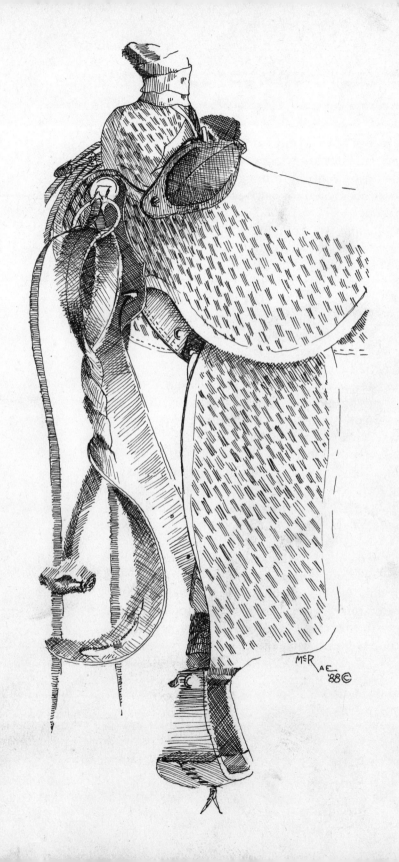

# COWBOY CURMUDGEON (C. C.)

I got a diploma 'cause I went to school.
They give me a letter for ridin' a bench.
But pieces of parchment don't prove you're no fool
'N my thirst fer knowledge was easy to quench.
I don't own a medal from fighting no war.
I never been cited for valor or dash.
What buckles I own was bought at a store,
Ain't champeen of nothin'.  I won 'em with cash.
My profile ain't noble.  I'm tendin' t'ward fat.
I can't play a gitar when singin' a song.
And folks think there's nothin' that I'm damn good at.
Well I'm here to tell ya' they're grievously wrong.
They call me a cowboy curmudgeon, you see.
The sound of it raises goose bumps on my back.
If you could decree the degree of C.C.
On me, I'd never cut anyone slack!
I thought for a while I'd be "iconoclastic"
And "Critical Rancher," yes, that crossed my mind.
But icons are scarce, or of late made of plastic
And "Cowboy Curmudgeon's" alliterative inclined.
So bring me your tired huddled mass of buffoons,
Your woodsy owl wise guys that can't find their trees.
I'll punch line the dudes and I'll poke their balloons
With my cudgel of cowboy curmudgeonese.
You lookin' for candor?  Well, canned you done got.
I'll wash all the wishys 'n hang 'em up high.
You're yearnin' for truth?  Well like it or not,
I'll render your gizzard and show it the sky.
So thank you, my critics, and few friends as well,
I'm trompin' in cow country sour grapes, you see.
I cherish the mantle.  And I'll give her hell
As Cowboy Curmudgeon.

McRae, The C. C.